P9-AFO-955

Person's Guide!

Beating overeating

The Lazy Person's Guide!

Beating overeating

Gillian Riley

Newleaf

Newleaf

an imprint of
Gill & Macmillan Ltd
Hume Avenue
Park West
Dublin 12
with associated companies throughout the world
www.gillmacmillan.ie

© Gillian Riley 2001
0 7171 3269 2
Design by Vermillion Design
Illustration by Emma Eustace
Print origination by Linda Kelly
Printed by ColourBooks Ltd, Dublin

This book is typeset in Rotis Semi-Sans 10pt on 13pt.

The paper used in this book comes from the wood pulp of managed forests. For every tree felled, at least one tree is planted, thereby renewing natural resources.

A CIP catalogue record for this book is available from the British Library.

5 4 3 2 1

CONTENTS

INTRODUCTION

THREE QUESTIONS

Welcome to a wonderful journey. This will be an adventure, and just like all adventures it will be challenging, risky and full of surprises. At times you might think you'll never get anywhere and that nothing will ever change. At other times you might fear so much will change you won't be able to handle it. Just stay with it and watch what happens. Let those thoughts and fears come and go. Get some support with it if you want to, someone to talk to about it all. I know you want *something* to change, otherwise you wouldn't be reading this book in the first place. So you've already started the journey. Just don't give up on it, however long it takes, and you will get there in the end.

First things first. You want to change something about the way you are with food, so that you can be more in control of what you eat. Now, in order to change your actions, you need to change the way you think. Why? Because behind every action there's always a thought. The thought can be ever so subtle, so subtle you may not even notice it, but it's there. You think, 'Another slice of cake looks good', and before you know it, you've eaten it. What you can do here is to learn a new way of thinking so that you can then change your actions. Then, you have the opportunity not to eat that other slice of cake.

When it comes to changing the way you think about food, there are just three things to keep in mind. Let's call them themes.

I'm going to describe what they are, so you can understand and remember them. Then, whenever your eating is not what you would like it to be – you're eating too much, or too much of the wrong things – you ask yourself about these three themes.

Whenever any one of them is out of place, you'll feel out of control with food in some way. You'll be eating too much or too often or the wrong things at the wrong times. When you question yourself about these three themes and find the truth about them for yourself, then you'll be able to gain control of your eating. Then, you can feel at peace with food. Then, you have a good relationship with food. Then, willpower is an asset you naturally employ when it comes to what you eat and how much you eat.

So what are these three questions? I'll list them here and then I'll go into more detail over the following chapters:

1. Am I Choosing?

It's tough to stay in control of overeating when you forget to make your own free choices. If you ever notice a rebellious quality to your eating, especially if you feel completely out of control at times, this is the theme for you to tackle. Or, if you feel deprived when you don't eat something, this is the theme for you. When you learn how to eliminate the rebelliousness and the feelings of deprivation, then you can take control. Then you can make free choices using the power of your free will.

2. What's My Motivation?

Here we look at why you might make one choice over any other. For example, you might ask yourself, 'Why don't I eat some more cake?' Or, 'Why am I eating an apple for my snack instead of a chocolate bar?' We always have reasons for the things we do, but often we lose sight of what they are. In Chapter 2 we'll see how your motivation can be made more effective.

3. How Am I Responding To Temptation?

This theme addresses your desire to overeat; the urge, impulse and attraction toward all that extra food you don't really need. In the past you may have tried to control this by distracting yourself, keeping occupied with something else so that you don't feel tempted. But temptation rarely leaves for ever, so success gets compromised. You can begin to think differently about feeling tempted and about feeling satisfied. When you do, the magic really starts to happen. This book shows you how.

Is it really this simple? Well, yes and no. It is simple in that all you need to remember is these three themes and the questions. It isn't simple in that you need to be honest with yourself, so that you don't deceive yourself with false answers. A counsellor – anyone who can listen to you in a supportive way and give you straight and honest feedback – can help. It takes time, effort and courage to change the way you think, but it really is possible, for anybody. And you can go as fast or as slow as you like.

WHAT YOU CAN DO

■ *Keep it private.* Over the next few chapters you'll see how to access and develop a powerful and very practical sense of choice about food. When you start practising with these ideas, it's best to keep it to yourself as much as you possibly can. Think about this by yourself, without explaining or discussing what you're doing as part of your everyday conversations. Talking to a counsellor, support person or support group is fine, but as much as possible keep all your discussions about eating and weight within those designated meetings and conversations.

This advice goes doubly if you have someone in your life who puts any pressure on you to control your eating and lose weight. If there's someone who makes comments about your size or comments on what you eat, that is especially the person you don't want to get involved in what you're learning here. They may well continue to make their comments, but you don't have to respond to them; so don't take the bait – and try changing the subject whenever you can.

Of course you'll need to make some decisions with others sometimes: what the family will have for dinner, perhaps, or what restaurant your group of friends will go to. But exactly what and how much you eat is up to you and is best decided by you. So, for example, if you want a second helping of something, you don't talk about it. You learn how to think it through for yourself and make a private decision about whether or not to have it.

This can be tough to do if you are used to talking with others about what you are or are not eating. You'll need to train your friends and family, to get them used to the 'new you' who isn't going to think out loud about food and how you feel about eating or not eating it.

Later on, when you've spent a while working with this book, you may want to talk about some of it with people close to you. You'll know when you're ready to do that, and you'll know by then that it's still best not to talk about it when you're eating.

■ *Keep it simple.* One of the best things about this approach is that you don't need to make other changes in your daily life in order for this to work. Taking control of overeating doesn't depend on whether you have a wildly exciting social life or are lonely and isolated. It doesn't depend on whether you're standing up, sitting down, watching TV or driving. It doesn't depend on whether you're at work or at home. Unemployed or bringing up children. Happy and productive or depressed and bored.

You can learn how to control what and how much you eat no matter what is going on in your life. And the best thing about this is that you don't need to wait until other things in your life change before you can make changes in your eating. You can get to work on it right away, just as things are. In fact, working on things just as they are right now is the best way to proceed. You'll see why later on in the book.

■ *Let it in.* The first time you read this book you'll begin to understand the principles, but you're only going to get good results if you can let these ideas become real to you. It may take reading this book a couple of times before some of it begins to sink in enough to make a difference. This doesn't mean you are a slow learner, or that you will never learn anything here that will really give you control. It's just the way it is for most people. It takes a while, and this means you need to be a bit persistent. First of all you understand these ideas; but then you need to live them, by bringing them into the daily thoughts you have about food.

It's likely you'll come across some things that are tough to hear, truths you'd rather not face and facts you'd sooner ignore. You can do that but it won't work as well. So it may take a while before you can let down some of your guard and really let it in. Take it at your own pace. Get some support with it if you want to. Keep returning to this book, and eventually you'll be able to own it in a way that enables you to break through the barriers and access the power you already possess to take control. Then, things will change. Not just for a while but in real, lasting ways. Not because you read a book, but because you changed the way you think about food.

Gillian's Story

My own progress with food has been gradual over a number of years, not at all dramatic but none the less valuable. I certainly eat a good deal less than I used to and the quality of what I eat has improved beyond recognition. I've made these changes in exactly the ways I describe in this book. I've certainly got the potential to be quite indulgent with food. I enjoy my food very much, but I really enjoy being able to stop, too.

For me, a healthy relationship with food is about consuming things I need as much as it's about not consuming other things I don't need. I know it's not like this for everybody, but it's incredibly easy for me to avoid eating fresh fruit and drinking anything like enough water every day. Very often I find that when I eat the foods I need, it becomes easier not to eat the things I don't.

I write not only from my own experience but as the result of all I've learned over years of running courses on taking control of overeating. People come to the sessions, which are held once a week, and we talk these things through. Then they go through their daily lives and come back the following week to talk about what worked and what didn't. This book contains the experiences, the questions and the answers that have come out of this process. Much of what you read here is exactly what we have discussed during these evenings.

Every time I lead a course, I meet a new group of people and I learn more about what people need to understand so they can take control with food. There's always a wide range of difficulties, because everybody's different, but there are also themes I notice over and over again. Not with everybody, but consistently enough so that I can see their relevance. I know they will help you for no other reason than that they have helped so many of those who have attended my courses. Some of those people have contributed their comments at the ends of the chapters that follow. It may help you to see these ideas expressed in other people's words.

CHAPTER 1

AM I CHOOSING?

Whenever you try to control what you eat, what kinds of things do you say to yourself? Do you think anything like this?

'I mustn't eat between meals.'
'I've got to stop eating these nuts.'
'I can't eat anything with sugar.'
'I'm not allowed to eat wheat.'
'Don't you dare eat any more of those.'

This style of thinking is very, very common, so I wouldn't be at all surprised if these thoughts or something like them go through your head whenever you try to control your eating. Sometimes they flash by very quickly, so it takes a bit of attention to catch them and realise that this is how you try to limit what you eat. Some people, though, gave up any attempt to control themselves so long ago that they've banished these thoughts completely and just go ahead and eat anything they fancy. If this is so for you, see if you can become more aware of your thoughts as you practise with the ideas in this book. It might be that you can spot this style of thinking after you've been overeating:

'I've got to stop eating so much.'
'I shouldn't eat so much junk food/fried food/chocolate/etc.'

'I won't eat any more chocolate for the rest of the week.'
'I must start that diet tomorrow.'
'I can't go on like this.'

Most people try to control their eating like this, by thinking in terms of commands, threats, rules, restrictions and prohibition. They think like an authority figure, a stern parent inside their own heads, shouting out orders. The harder they try, the louder this voice shouts at them, judges them and tries to bully them into submission.

This is what most people think of as willpower. It's no wonder they usually say they don't have any! I know I wouldn't want any of that. It sounds like a nightmare to me. In fact, it isn't willpower. It's the opposite of willpower and that's why it doesn't work – and it doesn't work, does it? If it did, you'd be out there obeying the orders, always being 'good', following the rules, never overeating or eating anything that's bad for you. The reality is more likely to be that the more you try to restrict yourself, the more you rebel and eat all the more.

You might be one of those people who can go along with restrictions for a while, perhaps when you're on a diet. You think along the lines of 'I am allowed to eat these things' (whatever's on the diet) and 'I'm not allowed to eat those things' (maybe just a few but not a lot of those things because they aren't on the diet). It works for a while, but you know from experience that it doesn't last. At some point it all falls apart. Rebellious, out-of-control overeating kicks in again, you're eating even more than when you first started, and you keep putting off returning to the diet because it feels so restrictive. You think, 'I'll do that diet again one day, but not today. I'm too busy to think about it right now.' And so you go on, wishing you had some willpower with food.

The problem, you see, is created by thinking in terms of following rules and restrictions. Thinking this way creates a devastating feeling which will always undermine your best intentions. This feeling is the sense of deprivation which destroys your attempts to control what you eat.

Feelings of deprivation are an adult version of the temper tantrum a child throws when it wants something and is being prevented from getting it. This temper tantrum means you're going to be upset until you get what you want. You might think you don't go as far as throwing tantrums over food, but see if you don't throw a sophisticated, ever-so-subtle, adult version – an adult version which is just as deadly as the tantrums you see in the supermarkets from the toddlers with their exasperated mothers.

These deprivation tantrums can be so fleeting they're gone in a second. It can be the briefest glimpse of martyrdom, just at the thought of not eating this particular thing you fancy. This feeling is so negative, it need do no more than threaten to appear. This threat is the fear that if you don't eat this thing NOW you're really going to regret it. You aren't going to stop thinking about it, you'll eat something else that's even worse to compensate yourself, and when you do get your hands on some, you'll eat ten times as much. You've got yourself over a barrel. You're damned if you do, but you're even more damned if you don't.

This is the nightmare so many people live with. They want to eat less, and especially less of certain things, but when they are attracted to these foods their willpower is nowhere to be found.

It's been wiped out by the feeling of deprivation, even by the fear of it. Eliminate the feeling of deprivation and you can access your willpower.

I realise you may just need to take my word for it at this point, because you don't have your own experience to test this out yet, but what I want to explain to you in this chapter is that deprivation is created by a state of mind. It's an attitude, a way of thinking. The feelings of deprivation are created when you deny your freedom of choice, and you deny your freedom of choice by thinking in terms of commands, threats, rules, restrictions and prohibition. Check out the sentences at the beginning of this chapter and see if any of them don't ever flip through your head. They leave you feeling as if you're being bullied. Like you've been put in prison, forced to eat rabbit food, and there's no way out.

Loss of freedom can be one of the most devastating things that can ever happen to a human being. This is true of any freedom that's rightfully yours: freedom of speech, for example, or the right to vote, or the right to worship. These and many more are all freedoms most of us take for granted, but we would object strongly if they were ever taken away. We also have every right to eat whatever is ours to eat – and that's the freedom you deny when you tell yourself you 'can't', 'have to' and 'must'.

This is why it's the opposite of willpower. Willpower is the power of your will, and your will is free. When you deny free choice, you deny your free will. Then, you can't possibly use the power of your will.

The solution is contained in the power of choice. When you choose, you access your will. In order to genuinely choose, you need to know you've got choices, that you're completely free to eat anything and everything you might want. Everything changes when you get this and everything falls into place behind that. You don't feel deprived, you don't need to do any rebellious overeating and you find you have a far greater sense of control.

It's very straightforward and it turns everything on its head. Free choice. The rule is that there are no rules. All you need to do is get used to thinking in a different way. It's really that simple. What's not so simple is putting this into action, because it takes some repetition to get it to sink in and become a reality for you.

As well as repetition, it may also take facing up to a fear which can block your path. This fear is that if you really let yourself believe you're completely free to eat anything – you will! That's why you deny choice in the first place. It can take time to overcome this fear, to let in a genuine sense of freedom around food and to own the choices you make. Owning your choices fully means choosing the complete picture – including the consequences!

Are you thinking you've heard all this before? I've often come across advice about making sure you don't deprive yourself of anything, so it's possible this is sounding a bit familiar. The advice I'm talking about is usually 'to eat whatever you want but in moderation', and the idea is that then you won't feel deprived. That's not what I'm saying here – and it's important to understand the difference.

Perhaps you are already aware of the flaw in the standard advice. Setting out 'to eat what you want but in moderation' is all very well unless eating in moderation leaves you feeling deprived! After all, it is the immoderate amount you eat that you're trying to control in the first place, isn't it? The problem for most people is that eating enough to never feel deprived means overeating, and especially it means eating things that are bad for your health.

What I'm suggesting is something else completely: that the difference between feeling deprived or not is in whether or not you genuinely believe you are choosing. You feel deprived when you forget that you are the one who is choosing, as if you've got the bad end of the deal. The difference is in your attitude, your frame of mind. It has nothing to do with what and how much you are eating. It's entirely possible not to eat for long periods of time and not feel deprived. It's entirely possible to feel tempted by food, but not eat it and still not feel deprived. The reason you don't feel deprived is because you're remembering that it's your choice.

This of course takes some effort on your part. This isn't an instant, magic fix, but even starting to work with it will produce some results, and hopefully this will encourage you enough to want to continue. For most people, though, it does take a while to become real and more than just an interesting idea you once read about in a book.

Consider this, though. It might be that this is the only way you can ever develop control over your eating. This might be it! Perhaps there never will be a pill you can take, a magic formula or a saviour who will come along and sort out this problem for you. It could be that you either continue to think in ways which make the problem worse, however gradually, over the years of your life. Or, you start to make changes, however gradually, that lead to you living your life more as you want to: in control of what you eat, calmer, healthier and enjoying a stronger sense of self-esteem that enhances everything you do.

The key is to experience what a difference it makes in your relationship with food when you genuinely choose. When you do, that experience will be of great significance to you, because it will put everything into a different context. It works especially well if you have good reasons for the choices you are making. In other words, you know what is motivating you. If you have good motivation, you can make positive choices. That's what we'll look at in our next chapter.

WHAT YOU CAN DO

- *Remind yourself you have a choice* whenever you think about eating. Tell yourself, 'I can eat this,' or 'This is my choice,' whenever you eat anything. It's especially important to do this if you are eating in a compulsive way and you are feeling out of control. That is because you are then most likely to revert to prohibitive thinking, so it's good to counteract it and reconnect with a genuine sense of choice. This means recognising that you can go on bingeing, that you can overeat all your life and that you never have to stop. You've got these choices – whether you want them or not. Then, and only then, you can choose how you really want to live.

- *Whenever you're in a restaurant or food shop*, let yourself know that you can eat anything you want and as much as you want. And you can return the next day and eat even more. Then, choose what really works for you, remembering the consequences of your different choices.

- *Remind yourself of the consequences* included in the choices you are making. For example, 'I'm choosing to eat this tub of ice cream and to feel nauseous and guilty afterwards.' You are free to eat anything and everything – but you don't have a choice about what the consequences will be.

- *If you feel deprived* whenever you don't eat something you fancy, it's because you haven't yet created a genuine sense of freedom for yourself. You might be paying lip service to the idea, you might understand the theory of it, but you don't yet feel it and experience it as a reality. That's OK! This is where many people start. The challenge for you is to continue to reinforce the idea of choice, so that eventually it becomes real and part of the way you always think about food.

- *If you detect a rebellious quality to your eating*, the same thing applies. Rebellion is only possible when there's a rule or restriction in place. Nobody can rebel if they have complete freedom, so remove the restrictions in the way you think and the rebelliousness will disappear.

- *Discussing these ideas as little as possible* with the people in your life will give you a better sense of your own choices. If someone makes a comment about what you're eating or not eating, just refuse to get involved in a conversation about it and concentrate on your own process in private. It's your own thinking you want to concentrate on. No matter what anybody else says, it's your own thinking that makes the difference.

■   *When you ask yourself: 'Am I choosing?'* see if you feel and
     believe you are choosing, even when you're not eating
     something you want.

Miriam's Story

*I'm a mother of three, a wife and a manager of a software company. I
did Gillian's course about a year ago and my eating has transformed, I
would say. I do slide occasionally, but I have many very good weeks now.*

*I think the major thing that still grabs me is this thing about
choice. That's what made the most impact on me. I simply refused to
put myself back in prison by stopping dieting. I have noticed that I'm
choosing not to eat when before I would have eaten addictively. I'm
choosing to eat a lot fewer biscuits. I know now that it's my free
choice, that I can do it if I want to but I don't have to. I used to eat so
much simply because I thought I wouldn't be able to later on, so I
wanted to get as much in while I still could. It was as though I was
always on the verge of a famine.*

*I was completely caught up in the trap of repeatedly dieting and
bingeing, dieting and bingeing, for several years. I would go to
various kinds of diet groups and find myself eating frantically as soon
as I had been weighed. I used to have this thing about Sundays,
because I would always start my diet again on Monday and so I used
to eat all day Sunday. Today, it's Sunday and I'm just delighted about
the way I have eaten. I was thinking earlier I'd have some toast, and I
thought no, I'll wait for supper. It seems so normal to think that way
now and yet it was never like that before. There was always so much
struggle whenever I was thinking about food.*

It's had an effect on other things in my life as well. I'm more conscious when I say I've 'got to' do something. I didn't get it at first, but I now realise the things I take on are my choice, so it comes back to me when I think, 'Oh no, I've got to do all this.' I remember that it's my choice and then it isn't a burden. In general I like being busy, but often it gets too much. It's a much wider thing than just food.

The benefit to me is definitely in terms of self-esteem, and it's a huge relief not to be on that diet bandwagon. I really enjoy eating and I really enjoy feeling in control. I feel liberated. I'm going to make a cabbage salad this evening. I positively enjoy that sort of thing now.

CHAPTER 2

WHAT'S MY MOTIVATION?

I bet you've heard other people say it and you may have said something like it yourself: 'There's nothing wrong with my motivation – I want to lose weight more than anything in the world.' Everywhere you look – at your friends, at TV, in magazines – people are talking about weight. They say things like:

> 'I'm tired of living in this fat body.'
> 'This extra weight is making my life a misery.'
> 'I look at myself in the mirror and I'm depressed for the rest of the day.'
> 'If my scales say I've lost weight I'm happy but if I've gained I'm miserable.'
> 'If only I was thinner my life would be so much better.'
> 'I'd love to walk into a room and not feel self-conscious because of my size.'
> 'I've struggled with my weight all my life.'
> 'If I had the choice either to win the lottery or be thin, I'd rather be thin.'

Of course there's no shortage of solutions offered to help you lose, control or manage your weight. Diets, low-fat foods and slimming clubs all promise to take inches off your thighs and fat off your backside. The problem is *weight* and the solution is to *lose* it.

It seems so simple and yet, as you may know, very few people are actually succeeding. If present trends continue, in just a few years one in four women in Great Britain will be obese. Not just a bit flabby. Obese, which is about three stone overweight. Already half our population, both men and women, weigh more than is good for their health. It's just as bad across most of Europe and even worse in America. The pressure to be slim comes from every angle, yet we, together with most of the western industrialised nations, are getting heavier and heavier. That should be our first clue that something is very wrong. Maybe motivation to lose weight isn't as straightforward as it seems.

Why don't we start to think about this in a new way, because clearly the old ways aren't working? I'm going to suggest one change in attitude by first of all making an analogy.

Let's imagine that one day you walk into your kitchen and see to your horror that your kitchen floor is flooded with water, three or four inches deep. Now that's a problem for you, isn't it? You panic, grab a mop and bucket and try to get rid of the water, thinking, 'Oh dear, oh dear, all that dreadful water all over the place, how can I make it go away, it's so horrible and wet, and there's so much of it.' And you mop and mop and mop.

In the middle of all this, someone walks in and points out to you that over at the sink the tap is running, the sink is blocked and the water keeps pouring out. You can see what they're saying, but you don't care very much about the tap and the sink. What you really care about is your floor, so that's what you concentrate on, mopping up the floor and fretting about the water. You have some people coming round and you're afraid they'll see the floor and all that dreadful water. You can hide the tap and the sink behind a screen and they'll never know it's there, but they'll be disgusted if all that water is there on the floor. If only you could get the water cleaned up.

You worry about the water for a long time. Whenever you talk about this problem with your friends, you talk about the water on the floor. Whenever your friends talk to you about it, they ask about the water, how deep it is and how you are doing with the mopping. Weeks go by. Then months. Then years. The water is still there, getting deeper and deeper, and you get more and more worried about it as time goes on.

This story illustrates what happens when you focus on the effect of a problem, the water on the floor, instead of its cause, the running tap. The story may seem rather unrealistic, but the chances are that you too have spent most of your time wanting to change the effect of your problem instead of the cause. You've probably tried to 'mop up' your excess weight by dieting. You've set goals for yourself to lose weight, such as, 'I want to lose a stone before my summer holidays.' And you've seen success or failure by how much weight you lost or gained. In the analogy, you are chiefly concerned with the floor, trying to get it dry and gauging success by how dry or wet it is. You know there's a tap running somewhere, but it's not nearly as important, is it?

Clearly there's something here that we all know: in general, dealing directly with the cause of a problem is going to work much better than trying to take care of the effects. In the analogy, if you dealt with the cause by getting the tap and the sink to do the work they were designed for, in time the water would evaporate and it would be fairly easy to keep dry. In the same way, when you eat the food that your body was designed for, in time, the weight evaporates and the weight loss is fairly easy to maintain.

Do you think you've been trying to do this already? Maybe, but it's also likely that the main focus of your attention – what really matters to you – has been your weight. Glance back to the beginning of the chapter and see if you don't identify with those first statements about losing weight. That's what's motivating you, isn't it? Weight loss. Wanting to lose weight is very likely the main reason you're reading this book. No matter how much you want it, it's still a weak motivation because it keeps you locked into the effect of the problem. You're still trying to mop up the water. Endlessly. This is one of the main reasons so few people are succeeding, even though they want it so much.

Now when you think about it, dealing with the cause of a problem is the obvious answer; so, you might ask, why doesn't everybody just figure this out for themselves? There's a good reason for this. It's a factor that gets in the way, it's very common, and this factor is low self-esteem. It's low self-esteem that keeps you locked into wanting to lose weight and seeing the size and the shape of your body as the main problem. Low self-esteem means that making the switch from effect to cause, far from being obvious and simple, is in fact a huge challenge. This really is the key to understanding how to motivate yourself in a much more powerful way, so let's understand it a bit.

A great many people see their problem with *overeating* as a problem with *weight*, and the reason they do this is because their self-esteem is low, or at least not as high as it could be. Low self-esteem means that appearance, being slim or at least slimmer, is all that really matters. Very crudely put, it's like thinking something such as: 'I don't think very much of myself, but if I looked really good or at least better than I do now, I might convince myself and others that I'm OK and maybe worth having around.'

This creates an absolutely dreadful relationship with food. An extreme example is someone who eats a chocolate bar for lunch, a packet of crisps for dinner and wouldn't dream of sitting down to a 'square meal' because it has too many calories in it. That's extreme, but I wouldn't be surprised if you make many decisions about what you will or will not eat based on what you look like, rather than on your nutritional needs. When you do that, all food can become the enemy because it can make you fat, and the main reason not to eat poor-quality food or too much food is your appearance. This keeps your attention on the size and shape of your body, which is really about your fear of being judged or rejected by other people. It's poor motivation because it's based on fear; it reinforces the low self-esteem, which in turn reinforces this way of thinking.

You might think, as many do, that if only you lost weight, your self-esteem would improve because you'd feel proud of the way you looked. But it doesn't quite work that way, as many people who have managed to get to their ideal weight know only too well. I often hear people say they felt as miserable when they were skinny as when they were fat. Often they were surprised by that, because they thought that looking good would solve everything.

Sometimes, though, you hear people say, 'Yes, losing weight is wonderful, but it's not the most important thing; there's something even more rewarding for me about the way I'm living now! That's closer to what I'm getting at, and I want to suggest that the people who think like this tend to be more successful in the long term. What makes the difference is that they found ways to motivate themselves that aren't exclusively about how much they weigh and what they look like.

Don't get me wrong; there's absolutely nothing wrong with losing weight – assuming of course that you are overweight to start with. It's when you can put that to one side and discover other reasons to take control of your overeating that things really start to change. The reason they start to change is because you then begin to raise your self-esteem.

Raising your self-esteem isn't just a nice idea: it's essential to developing control with food. Lower self-esteem means lower willpower, which in turn reinforces the low self-esteem. Higher self-esteem means greater willpower, which in turn reinforces the high self-esteem. How do you get started? You fake it till you make it. You need to deliberately set out to raise your self-esteem, because it won't just descend on you one day as if by magic. Nobody can ever bestow self-esteem on you. It is, after all, the esteem in which you hold yourself. What works is to declare your own worth, and one of the most powerful ways to do that is in the choices you make about the food you eat.

It's a completely different way to motivate yourself and it's a way that's much more effective, especially over the course of a lifetime. It's about eating in a way that supports and enhances your emotional and your physical wellbeing. It's about correcting the balance from a situation where losing weight is everything to just having it be a factor, and maybe just a bonus. It's fine to have both kinds of motivation. Most of us do. We will always want to look as good as we can and there's nothing wrong with that at all. What makes the crucial difference is having both kinds of motivation in a good balance.

When you draw the focus of your attention away from trying to look better and towards looking after your health, you immediately start to boost your self-esteem. This is because you are affirming that you value yourself enough to give your body what's best for it. You motivate yourself toward having a healthy relationship with food rather than looking a certain way. You can have both. You can have the best of health and look great too, but if you prioritise genuine self-esteem you will connect with a far more powerful and enduring source of motivation. Then, the weight loss pretty much takes care of itself.

WHAT YOU CAN DO

■ *Identify any motivation that's anything other than weight loss.* It's not that losing weight is a bad thing, it's just that we need to correct an imbalance. This imbalance occurs because weight loss – what other people can see and judge us by – has become much too important in most people's minds. Is there anything you like about eating less, besides losing weight? Make the effort to notice how your life is better when you eat in healthier ways. Do you have more energy and vitality? Fewer colds or headaches? Better digestion or sleep? Do you notice that your self-esteem is higher? That you like the feeling of being in control?

It will help you to write these things down so you can remember them later on. Write as much as you can, with your own personal details. You could make notes by completing the sentence, 'I want to eat less because ..' It might take weeks of thinking about this before you can come up with complete answers, but every time you do you'll be developing stronger motivation.

■ *Take note of any signs of less than perfect health* you many have. You might be able to think of them as messages sent from your body asking you to make changes in what you eat.

■ *If appearance is your main motivation,* find ways to play it down so that you can bring it into a better perspective. Instead of setting weight-loss targets, aim to eat in a way that best supports your physical and emotional wellbeing. Whenever you think you'd like to weigh yourself, stay off the scales and remind yourself of those other benefits.

This won't come naturally at first, so it takes deliberate effort. Discuss your weight as little as possible, whether you've lost some or not. Refuse to join conversations about dieting and weight. If someone says something like, 'Oh, you look good, have you lost weight?' say as little about it as you can. Change the subject if you possibly can.

■ *Be especially careful any time you lose weight.* Have you ever lost weight and immediately started eating more? It's very common. Losing weight gets you attached to the effect again, taking you off track with the cause. This is one place where you can see just how counterproductive weight loss is as a motivation. Keep as quiet as you can about any weight loss, hiding it under baggy clothes and not mentioning it to anyone. Sounds crazy, doesn't it? But it works.

It's best to think of weight loss as a kind of anti-motivation that gets in the way of your true motivation, which is genuine self-esteem and health. It can make a big difference, because then you move from motivation that reinforces lower self-esteem to motivation that reinforces higher self-esteem. And it's high self-esteem that will continue to motivate you in the long term.

■ *If you want to lose weight for health reasons*, don't assume that this chapter has no relevance for you. This could be the case, but many people are well aware of the health hazard of their excess weight, and still their emotional attachment is to their appearance.

■ *Find ways to improve the quality of your meals.* Are you one of those people who have settled for a mediocre way of eating, telling yourself it's healthy when in fact it could be quite a bit better? Are you still counting calories? Start to think in terms of eating for nutritional needs. Counting calories means you are focused on weight loss. Caring more about the nutritional content of your meals means you are building your self-esteem.

■ *Make a note of everything you eat for a few days.* If you haven't ever done this before, it can be a brave and powerful step. Some overeaters see their problem in terms of weight because they are honestly unaware of just how much they eat. Break through this, if you are ready, by writing it all down as you go. Every time you eat something, just make a note of it. Later on, you can review your notes and you may be able to see it from a different perspective. It may be easier to do if you can make absolutely sure that nobody else will ever see your food diary. Some research has demonstrated that overweight people underestimate the amount they eat by as much as 800 calories a day, and honestly don't know they are doing it.

■ *When you ask yourself: 'What's my motivation?'* find reasons that don't relate to losing weight. It's best to use your own words, but here are some I've heard people in my courses mention: more confidence, feeling in control, greater enjoyment of food, less stress, more energy, better digestion, better sleep, clearer thinking and higher self-esteem.

Perhaps the best motivation of all could be to slow down the process of aging, to stay younger and healthier for longer in your life. You strengthen your self-esteem when you motivate yourself this way. Weight loss will follow and it is much more likely to last.

Martha's Story

Self-esteem is what clicked for me. I've been through a lot of traumas recently and I've been very low, and this has been a way forward for me. At the moment I'm clearing all the junk out of my house, throwing it all out, and that's all been part of it. So it's been a whole life change.

I know it's not about weight but I've lost a stone so far. I'm not completely happy with my eating but I'm not bingeing any more, so that's nice. I'd like to find better ways to cook vegetables and plan my menus ahead of time and I'm not doing that yet. I'm making things up as I go along, and too often that degenerates into lots of ready-made meals and sandwiches. So that's one of the things I still want to change.

The changes have been gradual and sensible and it's definitely lasting. I don't fear that suddenly I'm going to start bingeing again, day after day, like I used to. I may overeat once but it's not the end of the world. I know it won't mean going down that slippery slope into that scary out-of-control stuff. Overeating is just not OK with me. This new perspective on things has helped me sharpen up my eating so much. It's about honouring myself and the impact that has on everything and every aspect of my life. I feel so much better now; when I think about all of it I just feel good.

I joined a gym and started exercising but I found it so boring I didn't keep it up. Now I take the dog for a walk every day. A long walk, for about an hour, and I prefer that. I get up in the morning and take the dog out before I go to work. Sometimes in the evenings I can walk for hours.

I'm thinking about choices a lot more and when I get stuck with something in my life I'm much more likely to think, 'Do I really have to do this?' And often I don't. This doesn't mean I'm doing less. I'm feeling even more productive these days, and creative and on top of things in general. I'm doing things because I want to do them, not because I have to.

CHAPTER 3

HOW AM I RESPONDING TO TEMPTATION?

You might call it an impulse or an urge. You might call it a snack attack. You fancy something. You're wanting to eat when you know you're not hungry. You're wanting to go on eating when you've just finished a meal. It's happening in all those moments when you wish you had some willpower. Many people call it a craving. For reasons we'll look at in a moment, it's what I call an addictive desire to eat.

The chances are you think of your desire to overeat as an enemy, because it seems to make you eat despite your very best intentions. It seems to overpower you, so the only way you can think of to escape its power is to avoid it. So, if being alone brings it on, you make sure you're always busy. If eating out holds the most temptation for you, you stop going to restaurants. If you eat a lot in front of the TV, you turn it off and find other ways to fill your evenings. Eventually, though, your addictive desire returns and you try to satisfy it with an apple or a few carrot sticks. That doesn't really do it, though, because what you really desire is something much more sugary and creamy or oily and salty. So sooner or later you satisfy your addictive desire to eat yet again, as you wonder how you will ever be able to stop eating so much.

Most people know that running away from a problem does nothing to solve it and can even make it worse. Yet this is the very strategy they try to use to control their overeating. At first it seems to work, but it only works up to a point, and the reason it stops working is simply that it's impossible to avoid temptation for ever. Food is there in your life every day, almost everywhere you go, and a lot of it will tempt you – as if you didn't know that already!

So let's look at an alternative, because there really is another way of approaching this, a way that's completely different from anything you've ever tried before. It's such an unconventional solution, though, that this way may at first seem strange, impossible and even ridiculous. It may take a while before you can really grasp it – but when you do you'll find it works like a charm.

What I'm going to suggest is that you look at this addictive desire to eat and think of it as your friend instead of your enemy. Well, I did say ridiculous, didn't I? Just continue to read through this chapter and see if there aren't some things here that give you a glimpse that this may be possible. Just consider that if you did make friends with your desire to overeat, you wouldn't fear it and you wouldn't need to run away from it – but most of all, you wouldn't have to satisfy it. You'd feel genuinely tempted from time to time and you'd feel absolutely fine about that. Maybe sometimes you'd eat in response to that temptation, but you wouldn't have to. In this way you'd be able to keep yourself from eating so much, not because you'd avoided temptation but because you'd learned to live with it, happily and easily.

There are good reasons why I don't call it a craving. A craving is an intense and miserable experience, and you know from Chapter 1 that it's created by the state of deprivation. Cravings belong to the temper tantrum of the deprived child who wants something it can't have. When you create a feeling of free choice for yourself – and sometimes this needs to be recreated from time to time as you remind yourself of your choices – the intense cravings simply evaporate.

Not only that, but the word 'craving' doesn't describe much of the experience I'm talking about. An addictive desire to eat can be quite strong at times, especially when you're first working with this approach, but it can also be extremely subtle. Sometimes it's a simple thought, so brief it's almost unnoticeable. It can simply be, 'Oh yes, I'd like some of that.' This is not what we usually think of as a craving, so I use the term 'addictive desire to eat' to include both the stronger feelings of desire and the fleeting thoughts.

It makes a huge difference to be able to identify even those brief thoughts of desire, because a great deal of overeating gets done in a fairly unconscious way. You may not be aware you are feeding an addictive desire, and maybe not too aware of what and how much you're eating either. It's impossible to control something you aren't aware of, so noticing and naming your desire to eat is a crucial first step. If you just think in terms of 'craving' you'll miss a lot of it.

Becoming aware of addictive desire is, of course, just the first step. It's a hugely significant step, but even when you've named it you're still wanting to eat something. You need to handle this experience so that you've got the option not to satisfy your desire, or at least not to satisfy it quite so often. This is where we get back to that idea of making the desire your friend.

As with any friendship, understanding goes a long way towards making friends. Theories have been put forward in a number of books that the reason people want to eat too much is to do with their biochemistry. It's their hormones, brain chemicals such as serotonin and dopamine, blood sugar and insulin levels or nutritional deficiencies that make them feel an addictive desire for more food. These can play a part – but our minds are far more powerful than all of these factors put together.

Essentially, an addictive desire to eat is a thought, and the best way to describe it is as a memory. It's the memory you have of eating addictively in the past. It's easy to check this out in your own experience. If you have a snack every time you go to bed, then getting ready for bed will remind you that it's snack time. If you eat every time you feel bored, then every time you feel bored you'll want to eat something. If you buy a chocolate bar every time you pay for petrol when you fill your car up, you will inevitably desire your favourite snack every time you're there.

This is called the 'conditioned response' and was first demonstrated by the scientist Pavlov, who was investigating how salivation works. He rang a bell every time he fed his dogs and soon the dogs salivated whenever they heard the bell, thinking food was on its way. In much the same way, we train ourselves to associate food with all kinds of cues in our lives. And, as with the dogs, the response can also be physical.

This is why your addictive desire to eat can at times be felt as a sensation in your body. Body and mind are powerfully connected, in communication with each other all the time, so thoughts often show up as physical feelings. For example, the thought 'Oh my God, I've locked my keys in the car!' can produce an undeniable sinking feeling in the stomach. In the same way, the thought of wanting to eat something may show up as a sensation of emptiness, not entirely unlike hunger.

Well, maybe it is hunger, I hear you say. Not if you've just finished a meal, it isn't. That's your addictive desire to eat, simply you thinking you want more. It's your thought that wants to be satisfied, not your body. This is why you can sometimes eat and eat and eat and eat and eat and never seem to satisfy this addictive appetite.

The addictive desire isn't just any memory, though: it's a memory of something pleasurable and satisfying. This gives it that extra bite as a memory, makes it more compelling and explains why it's experienced as a desire rather than an impartial recollection. When you eat a meal you inevitably experience pleasure and satisfaction, and that's why you'll often end a meal with a desire for more.

Understanding that your addictive desire is an inevitable memory helps you to accept it as part of your life. It doesn't mean you are mad, bad or greedy. It doesn't mean you're doing anything wrong and that you need to do something – go into therapy or find exactly the right diet – to make it go away. It simply means you have eaten addictively in this circumstance in the past and you have a memory of that. You've got choices, but one choice you don't have is to erase your memory. You either reinforce this memory or you leave it unsatisfied. If you leave the addictive desire unsatisfied, you get to be in control of your overeating as a direct result, and in time it fades.

You may be thinking that it's going to be tough to make friends with something that seems to control you. You may know that the addictive desire can put you into a kind of trance, when you want to eat so much that all other thoughts disappear from your mind. You forget why you wanted to stop eating so much. You forget how good you feel when you eat more wisely. You get mesmerised by desire and all you can think about is food.

When you avoid temptation and this feeling of desire, you never learn how to get out of this trance state, so you're always going to be its victim when it's there. Far more powerful is to develop the skill of talking yourself through it, by turning around to face it and deal with it. At first, though, even when you do face it, you may still fight it and struggle with it, simply because you hate it and really you just wish it would go away. This actually makes things worse, because the more you fight something, the more it's going to fight back.

You stop fighting your addictive desire to eat by accepting it, so that it simply flows through you without any opposition. You let yourself relax into the feeling and let the desire to eat be there. This doesn't necessarily mean that you're enjoying it. It is, after all, an uncomfortable sensation. It simply means you are willing to feel it. You learn how to think yourself out of, and break, the trance by paying attention to it and choosing to let yourself experience it.

Accepting it makes things a lot easier. It's best to accept it unconditionally, but mostly you'll find that if you really are choosing it and you really are accepting it, it doesn't hang around for nearly as long. There may be a few days, especially at first, when it's there a lot, but this diminishes over time. It's a paradox: the more you genuinely accept it, the more it fades.

Accept it by thinking of this uncomfortable feeling as the price you pay for the control that you want to gain over food. If someone offered you a fortune to accept feeling your addictive desire just once, I wouldn't be surprised if you'd do it. So, it's just a matter of figuring out for yourself whether what you're really going to get is worth it to you. What you get isn't a fortune in money, but the good fortune of the quality of your life when you are eating less. That is exactly how you take control of overeating, by re-evaluating your priorities. You can only do that while you are feeling your unsatisfied addictive desire to eat.

It's impossible to learn how to swim without being in some water. It's impossible to learn how to drive without getting into a car. In the same way, you will not be able to learn how to take control of your overeating until you let yourself experience your addictive desire to eat and learn how to talk yourself through it.

I find this concept is often quite a difficult thing for people to really understand, but makes the biggest difference when they do. Often people will make all kinds of plans about how they are going to eat more sensibly, but they forget about their addictive desire. Then, when temptation strikes, their plans are forgotten and they are left wondering why they didn't follow through. It's fine to want to make changes, to have an intention, for example, to eat less bread. Just remember that the choice doesn't actually get made until you're wanting your mid-morning toast snack. It's how you deal with that experience of addictive desire that makes all the difference.

Of course it's crucial to know it's your own free choice, but often people think in terms of choosing either to eat or not to eat something. So they think, 'Shall I eat the toast or not?' That's certainly the result, but it's not the best way to think about it. It's much better to put powerful words to the process, because by describing it correctly you create an entirely new attitude towards eating.

The best way is to think to yourself, 'Right now I'm feeling an addictive desire to eat.' Even if that's as far as you go, that will be something, but you don't have to stop there. Then, you can say, 'Yes, I'm willing to feel this. Yes, it feels uncomfortable but I'd rather have this feeling than spend the rest of my life overeating. It's worth it to me to feel this because it means I get back my health and my self-esteem.'

The more you make your choices in this way, the easier it will become and the more natural it will seem. You make the addictive desire your friend, because by accepting it as part of your life you get to break free from overeating and all that goes with it. You let it live with you because by doing so, as a direct result, you can control what and how much you eat. You accept it because it will change your life. It could even save your life.

This is about facing the difficulty of making a genuine, lasting change in your relationship with food. This is about dealing with this problem in everyday, practical experience. This is about using the power of your free will. You choose, and the way you choose is either to satisfy your addictive desire to eat or to accept it by being willing to feel it. Fundamentally, those are the choices that are open to you.

So that you can become even more aware of this addictive desire, let's look briefly at what it isn't. To complicate things, it's possible to feel an addictive desire at the same time as these other kinds of hunger:

Natural Hunger, a feeling of emptiness in your stomach, is a natural signal from your body telling you it's time to eat. It will come and go, and although it's wise to eat something soon, you don't feel compelled to eat unless it's accompanied by addictive desire. In fact you can feel perfectly happy, energised and alert when your body isn't being overworked by digesting food all the time. If your natural hunger feels physically painful, this may be from over-acidity, and it may be a good idea to consult a doctor.

Natural hunger can be quite difficult to identify, especially for people who overeat often. It can go missing when logic tells you it really should be there, and it can seem to be there when you wouldn't expect it, when you've just eaten something. This of course is addictive hunger, but it can feel just like the real thing.

Not only is natural hunger tricky to spot, but waiting until you are genuinely hungry before you eat can be extremely inconvenient, especially when you need to fit in meal times with other people. Sometimes you may have something to do (like work!) where it's not practical to stop and eat later on. You need to schedule meals around other commitments, but it's not easy to schedule natural hunger, which may or may not have surfaced before one o'clock when you need to run your errands, teach a class or attend a meeting.

You may have been advised in the past to eat only when you feel naturally hungry. In principle there's nothing wrong with this advice, but for many people it's virtually impossible to carry out. Some people get into difficulty with food simply because they continually fall short of this impossible goal. This is why it's best to just think ahead about when you aim to eat again. The more you can identify and accept your addictive desire to eat, the easier this will become.

False Hunger is a sign that something is physically wrong, that your eating has started to affect your health. False hunger makes it difficult to stay in control of your eating, so it's important to understand and correct this situation. There are two causes: acid indigestion and low blood sugar, and you might be prone to one or both of these.

Acid Indigestion can be very painful and many sufferers often overeat simply to make it go away. Even the fear that you might get hungry later on is likely to cause you to overeat, so that you won't feel the pain of an empty acid stomach. Antacid medications are bad for your health if you take them regularly, so it's much better to correct the problem directly.

Alcohol and caffeine contribute to over-acidity, but cigarettes are the biggest cause. As for food, nutritionists recommend a balance of 20 per cent acid-forming foods (meat, poultry, fish, eggs, grains and cheese) with 80 per cent alkaline-forming foods (most vegetables and fruits). Also helpful is to keep sugar and wheat to an absolute minimum, as they are very common contributors to an overly acid body, and to take regular exercise and plenty of water. Acidity can lead to very serious problems such as ulcers, rheumatism and arthritis, so it's important to deal with this, quite apart from eliminating this cause of false hunger.

Low Blood Sugar comes from the rapid rise and fall of insulin and glucose in the bloodstream caused by overeating certain kinds of carbohydrates. This connection between carbohydrates and insulin and glucose release is rated by what is known as the 'glycemic index'.

Carbohydrates that trigger a strong response of insulin and glucose are are said to have a 'high glycemic index'. It's no coincidence that these are mostly foods which people tend to eat addictively and have difficulty controlling. They provide a drug-like 'fix' but, like most drugs, they let you down soon after. This let-down, the low blood sugar, is a major cause of false hunger. Carbohydrates with a high glycemic index include: breakfast cereals, rice cakes, wheat bread and crackers, popcorn, most rice, pitta bread, pastry, cakes, croissants, potatoes in any form, bananas and anything which contains refined sugar or glucose.

Carbohydrates that cause insulin and glucose to be released more moderately are rated as having a 'low glycemic index'. They provide the body with sustained energy and mental alertness, and include rye, oats, green vegetables and most fruits.

If you often feel hungry, irritable or drowsy during the day, especially mid-morning, late afternoon or soon after eating, low blood sugar may be the reason. Here is an example which has come up a few times in my courses. Someone eats what they consider to be a substantial, healthy breakfast of cereal or wheat toast, but gets so hungry by mid-morning they have great difficulty waiting until lunch time before they eat again. Eating a larger breakfast doesn't make things any better. Eating low glycemic index carbohydrates for breakfast – oats, rye toast and fruit for example – makes all the difference.

If you experience these sudden and otherwise inexplicable drops of energy, think back to what you last ate and see if it included high GI carbohydrates. Your brain needs a lot of glucose to function well, so you'll probably feel sluggish mentally as well.

If false hunger is a problem for you and you take measures like this to eliminate it, you are just left with your addictive desire to eat. This desire, of course, is much easier to deal with when you aren't experiencing the false hunger as well.

WHAT YOU CAN DO

- *Notice your addictive desire to eat* so that you can gain the awareness you need to take control. Only when you've identified it and named it can you make a choice about it. If you aren't aware of it and what it is, it will run you.

  At first, it may be difficult to identify, so try setting a time goal so that your addictive desire will stand out more clearly. Setting a time goal means you agree with yourself that you intend not to eat until a certain time. Do this especially during those times of day when you want to take control of snacking or 'grazing'. Make sure you don't fall into a state of deprivation, so remind yourself you always have the choice to eat, even before you get to your chosen time.

- *Allow yourself to feel your addictive desire*, because this is how you take control. One place it's sure to show up is at the end of a meal. Have a clear picture in your mind of what you intend to eat before you start. When you finish the amount you planned, the chances are you'll want to go on, and this is your addictive desire. You can practise accepting this desire at the end of meals.

- *End your meals feeling unsatisfied.* Sometimes you hear

advice to 'eat until you're satisfied', but this doesn't take the addictive desire into account. There are people who don't have an addictive relationship with food who really do eat until they're satisfied and it's not a problem for them. Most people, however, do feel an addictive appetite after a meal. If you try to satisfy your addictive desire, you'll be overeating. You probably won't feel satisfied until you've overeaten so much that you're both physically and psychologically uncomfortable, much too full and guilty and maybe even panicky about the binge you just went through. That puts an end to your feeling of addictive desire, but when those adverse feelings let up, the addictive desire returns and you're overeating again. Allowing yourself to feel unsatisfied is your way out of this nightmare.

■ *Notice the difference between an enjoyment of food,* which is both positive and appropriate, and the 'high' you get from satisfying your addictive desire. It's important to enjoy what you eat, but some people eat so much highly addictive food – mostly sugar, wheat, salt and fats – they lose their taste for fruits and vegetables. Junk food satisfies your addictive desire. Real food satisfies your nutritional needs. They are quite different experiences and it will help you a lot to tell them apart, especially if you tend to justify overeating by thinking, 'I really enjoy my food – what's wrong with that?'

■ *There may be no need to abstain* from your 'binge' or 'trigger' foods. Whenever you eat your favourite 'drug', be it sugar, chocolate, nuts, bread or whatever, your addictive desire for them may be awakened. It might be easier for you to cut them out completely, but abstinence can be unrealistic and not at all necessary once you learn how to deal with addictive desire. It's important to eat in a way you feel you can live with, to have some flexibility and variation.

■ *When your favourite foods are available to you,* you're likely to feel more of a desire for them. It might be better not to have some things in the house because they drive you too crazy, so find what works best for you. At least be aware that by having certain things around you, your addictive desire for them may be far more persistent. You might find it works better to accept your addictive desire for them when you're in the supermarket, so that you can leave them there on the shelves.

■ *Remind yourself why* you are accepting this desire by thinking of what you gain by not overeating. Look for reasons other than weight loss and make sure they are your own, selfish reasons. It may be the energy you gain or it may be the sense of freedom, control or accomplishment. Just have it be something for yourself, something that's a joy to you in your life. Then it makes sense for you to accept the uncomfortable feeling of desire, because the trade-off is a good one.

■ *An intense or persistent craving* is a sure sign you're feeling deprived, and it's vital you change your way of thinking so that it doesn't wear you down. If you're feeling deprived it's because you've forgotten that you've got choices, or maybe that you're just paying lip service to the idea without really believing it. You might hold out until a good excuse comes along, but when you feel deprived you're likely to create a good excuse if one doesn't show up on its own. Chapter 1 will help you to turn this around.

■ *Don't be put off* by the word 'addiction'. It simply refers to all the food you eat that you don't actually need. Mostly, it's enjoyable, available, common and thoroughly integrated into our lives and our thoughts. There is a biochemical side to addiction, but it doesn't have the last word on what actions you will take. Certain kinds of food, especially sugar, processed grains, salt and fat, have an effect on our biochemistry. This is why they tend to have a more addictive quality to them. In other words, it's very easy to eat them far too much. When you cut them out, you experience withdrawal. If you make dramatic changes in your eating, which by the way isn't required, you can experience symptoms of detoxification, which is the physical withdrawal. Your addictive desire to eat, which is what this book is all about, is the psychological withdrawal.

■ *Ask yourself: How am I responding to temptation?* and see where and when you are feeling your addictive desire and what you are doing about that. Begin to make choices to accept this desire to eat as a trade-off for the benefits which come from eating less. The more you do that, the less you will be overeating.

Karen's Story

I had been obese for almost ten years and I had high blood pressure and a strong fear that I would become diabetic. I had talked about this with my doctor and she often warned me about my weight. I had dieted all my life and failed at it all my life. I felt really quite miserable about the whole thing. Nothing I did worked, but it wasn't for lack of trying.

I did a counselling course for years and went through endless hours of counselling in a determined effort to get to the bottom of my overeating. There were other issues too, and the counselling helped a lot with some of them, but my eating was always the main problem and the one that felt impossible to change. I always believed that if I could only find the root cause of my eating problem, find out what was behind it and heal that, then I would be able to stop overeating. This assumption, far from being challenged by the people running the course, was actively encouraged. For much of my life I carried around a strong sense that there was something wrong with me, something I could never discover and which my overeating continuously confirmed.

All that's changed now. When I did Gillian's course I kept waiting for the other shoe to drop, waiting for the cravings to return, but they never did. My addictive desire is in my mind and it's a completely different thing, nothing like I used to feel when I was dieting – or I should say, trying to diet. I never before had made the connection between what I ate and the state of my health. Before, it was always about weight, about how I looked. Now eating healthy foods and not eating unhealthy ones makes tremendous sense. It's all so obvious to me now, but you can get yourself into such amazing muddles about food and eating and weight.

The part of the course that remains with me most is about the addictive side of eating, because I now know what to do when I'm feeling 'hungry' – which of course isn't feeling hungry at all. It doesn't happen nearly as much as it used to; it's changed. I'm realising there are periods of time when I have this addictive hunger, and that I don't have to satisfy it.

At the moment I'm doing a 28-day detox, and it's very interesting because I'm not eating wheat. I hadn't realised how very 'moreish' bread was, and that's something that's really come home to me. I'm eating rye bread on this detox, so I'm still eating bread, but I'm not doing that continuous nibbling that I used to do with the regular bread.

CHAPTER 4

HOW TO GET A NEW BRAIN

Have you ever thought you'd need a new brain before you could be in control of your eating? I've heard people say this in my seminars. Well, guess what – you can get one! Not completely new (I expect there are a few bits you'd like to keep), but the part of your brain associated with wanting to eat can actually be physically altered! By you!

This may sound unbelievable, but is exactly what will happen when you follow the guidelines set out in this book. It's not really all that bizarre: in fact it's a natural process that happens to us all quite often. It just helps a lot to understand what it is you're doing so that you know why you are following a particular course of action. Then you can be more deliberate about it and therefore more effective. So that is what this chapter is about.

First of all, understand a very simple principle about how your brain works: that every cell in your brain communicates with other cells. Each cell does this by pulsing signals to the next brain cell which in turn signals to the next, setting off a chain reaction, one cell to the next, to the next, to the next, hundreds and thousands and millions of times across your brain. It's doing it right now!

There are billions of brain cells, so each signal could travel in an almost infinite number of directions. But they don't just scatter at random; the signals form patterns and these patterns form your familiar ways of thinking. This is how it happens. When two brain cells have pulsed their signals at the same time on several occasions, they connect chemically, so that when one of them now pulses it's much more likely to make the other one pulse as well. So, after a few repetitions of pulsing together, the cells team up into a partnership. In future they are much more likely to signal together, and this means you get to remember something. All of your memories and your knowledge are formed by these connections between the cells. The more you repeat any thought or action, the more these same cells get activated in the same pattern and the stronger their connection becomes.

Let's take an example. Let's say, every time you have a particularly tough day at work, you buy some biscuits and ice cream on the way home, and sit on your couch in front of the TV and eat them. The cells in your brain that remember 'it's been a tough day' are connected to 'biscuits and ice cream' (or maybe some sugary, creamy variation), and that's the memory you have and the connection you strengthen every time you eat this way after a tough day at work.

This is simplified of course, but is essentially how it works. We all know that repetition is our main tool for learning, whether learning to write, read, drive, play golf or whatever. Even if we just want to remember a phone number or the time of a train we want to catch, we learn things by repeating them over and over again.

The interesting part is how you go about changing things – assuming, of course, that you want to make a real change. The key is that when a particular pattern is no longer reinforced, the cells begin to disconnect. The connections don't disappear instantly, but do become weaker and weaker when that particular pattern of brain cell signalling is no longer activated.

So, you might think, why not change the whole routine and go out to a movie or the gym whenever you've had a bad day? Won't that weaken the connection? Not nearly as effectively as experiencing the inevitable memory of biscuits and ice cream connected to that situation. You might be accepting your desire for them as you pass by the shop where you would have bought them, and again when you're sitting in front of the TV. Either way, your conscious awareness of the process makes the crucial difference, so what works best is to pay attention so that you actively participate in rerouting the brain signals.

You could avoid the situation, whatever it is, but you don't change the patterns in your brain cells this way – and I bet you can check this out in your own experience. I wouldn't be surprised if, for some reason or other, you've avoided a situation in which you used to overeat, and when you returned to it you also returned to overeating. The reason for this is you never did weaken that particular brain connection between this situation and addictive eating.

This isn't nearly as difficult or complicated as it may sound. Remember it is happening in our brains anyway, as these connections between cells change and reform themselves constantly. Whenever we learn and remember something, new connections have been created in our brains. As we forget things, connections are made weaker.

The connections are usually not lost completely, though. Old memories can be stirred up from time to time, but this simply means you feel tempted again, although probably not as strongly. The addictive desire fades when you don't reinforce it, but some of that old connection always remains. You can tell this because it's usually easier to re-establish a link a second time than it was the first. So once it's been well established, it may always be that bit easier to fall back into old routines.

Phobias are treated, very successfully, in a very similar way. This is not to say you have a phobia: just that the process of recovery is similar. People can become phobic of almost anything, feeling overwhelmed and even paralysed with fear. The way this condition is treated is for the phobic person to gradually expose themselves to the feared object – a bird, for example. Their therapist might show them a drawing of a bird, then a photograph and later on perhaps a stuffed bird. Each of those stages will generate fear, and as the person allows themselves to feel and accept this fear it begins to fade. In time, they are able to go outside and see birds flying around without feeling so afraid. Eventually, they can be close to birds in a park and even feed them. In this way the brain patterns that connect 'birds' to 'fear' are weakened and the phobia is overcome.

In the same way, you expose yourself to feelings of addictive desire as and when they occur. When you're feeling your addictive desire to eat, when you want to eat more and you feel unsatisfied, those are the moments when real transformation takes place. This is because you then physically change the circuits in your brain.

Now, I'm sure you don't need me to tell you there are a great many connections in our brains associated with wanting to eat. If it was just bad days at work, that would be one thing, but we integrate addictive eating into our lives, so there are a great many things that trigger connections with food. You can breathe a sigh of relief here, because you don't need to face every single one of these connections in order to weaken them all. You'll work on some and others will seem to take care of themselves. However, there will still be many circumstances you'll meet for the first time which will form a powerful association.

For example, if you are someone who tends to eat whenever you're feeling a bit upset, you have established a connection between feeling upset and food, so every time you feel upset you'll want to eat something. You may not change this particular piece of brain circuitry unless you feel upset. It's only then that you get to rewire that connection. If you don't satisfy that desire, you begin to weaken the connection between feeling upset and eating. Then it fades. It doesn't go completely but it will be much less compelling. Simply avoiding anything that might upset you (as if you could!) doesn't do it.

Then there are the other connections, say, between eating and wanting to relax. And wanting to celebrate. And feeling sad. And visiting the local coffee shop (the one where they have those pastries). And walking into your kitchen. And going to the cinema. Etc., etc. Sometimes you get an addictive desire to eat for no other reason than that something just became available. You caught sight of it, smelled it or simply knew it was there, and now you want to eat it.

All you need to do about all this is continue to live your life as you normally do, and using the insights outlined in Chapters 1, 2 and 3, you develop the habit of noticing and making choices about your addictive desire to eat. It's not essential to identify the connection that triggered it. Sometimes it's obvious and sometimes it isn't. It can be a simple thought such as, 'What shall I do now? Oh, I think I'll eat something.' It can be the slightest feeling of annoyance about something or a vague sense of dissatisfaction.

By the way, you don't need to replace the eating with anything; in fact all this works much better if you don't, especially at first. It's not as if you're going to get a big hole in your brain where your addictive desire to eat used to be! You simply choose to accept these inevitable feelings of desire instead of satisfying them, and so you weaken them, and so they fade.

Knowing this can make a big difference, because it's very common for people to make lots of good changes in their eating, take control of their overeating and do very well for a period of time. Then, perhaps weeks or months later, they encounter a particular circumstance for the first time and they fall back into overeating again. The last time they were in this situation they overate, so there's suddenly a stronger connection, a sense of desire that has yet to fade.

For example, Mary lives with her family and rarely spends time alone. Then one day, all her family is away visiting a relative while she stays at home to get some work done. At the end of the day she feels a bit lonely and eats addictively. Mary explains it to herself as comfort eating, but another way to explain it is that she had a stronger addictive desire connected to a situation that she hadn't come across for a long time. Had she accepted this desire and not fed it, it too would have faded in time, even when she was on her own.

Unfortunately, it usually gets satisfied and reinforced, and what also gets reinforced is the sense of utter powerlessness to control eating in certain circumstances. So people say, 'I was doing fine until I went on holiday' or 'until I got stressed at work' or 'until I broke up with my boyfriend' or 'until I stayed at home all day with the kids'. Just remember that all these present nothing other than more brain connections that can be redesigned. As you go through these experiences in your life and no longer reinforce the connections with eating, they fade, just like any other memory.

Just as it's important to break these connections, it's essential to strengthen another kind of brain connection. This has to do with the theme of choice we discussed in Chapter 1. The connections associated with making choices have been identified by new brain-scanning technology which allows us to see live, moving pictures of brain activity in living people. A great deal of research is now being done using this technology, called a PET scan, and one experiment in particular highlights the impact of choosing.

In this experiment, volunteers lay in a PET scan doing nothing more than lifting one finger, while the researchers watched to see what parts of the brain were activated. First, they told the volunteers which finger to move and when to move it. Then, they let them decide themselves. There was a very clear difference between the two. As soon as the subjects started to make their own decisions, an area of their brain which had previously been inactive sprang into life.

This activity was in the prefrontal cortex, in a region which lies behind the forehead. It's the most adaptable part of the brain and it's the part that's the most highly evolved. This is where we keep our ability to choose for ourselves.

The action, moving a finger, was the same in both instances.

The difference was in choosing it rather than following orders. In the same way, you may actually eat less, perhaps while dieting, but do it by thinking you're following orders. Could it be that you aren't using that area of your brain? Does it matter? Well, it matters if you can develop this area physically when you actively choose, over and over again.

And this really is what happens. Particular areas of the brain develop as you use them. For example, professional violin players develop a much larger area of the part of the brain associated with the fingers that do most of the work. Their years of practice actually build and strengthen the connections in this area, which in turn enables them to perform even better. The same is true of others who use their fingers a lot, such as typists and blind Braille readers. As Braille is learned, the repeated stimulation of that one particular finger develops the brain area devoted to that finger. This is why people who read Braille can do so with one hand and not the other.

When the prefrontal cortex gets damaged through serious physical injury, people can lose control of their impulses. This kind of injury compels people to follow through on any whim that flips through their mind, and with impulses ruling absolutely, life is chaotic and relationships impossible. However, people with this kind of brain damage can become rehabilitated. Doctors have found that even physical damage can be repaired, and the ability to control impulse restored. This is carried out, not through surgery, but through deliberate, conscious repetition. Given half a chance, the brain rebuilds itself and restores itself.

Doctors who specialise in brain rehabilitation, after accidents or strokes for example, have found that two things make all the difference: *paying attention* and *repetition*. So, the more you deliberately choose, the more you activate and strengthen this area of your brain.

Inasmuch as you have difficulty with food, you've trained yourself not to control one particular kind of impulse, the impulse to eat. This training may have continued for years and may even have begun in childhood, before you had any idea what was happening. It wasn't a physical injury that impaired this particular brain function, but the effects could be similar.

You may still want to be impulsive around food sometimes, and that's fine. You'll want to eat spontaneously at times, but I'm assuming you're reading this book because you are way too impulsive around food and you have a tough time controlling that. The odd moments don't matter so much; it's the general picture we're working on here.

In general, you either strengthen the conditioning in your brain or you weaken it – all the time, every day, with every encounter with food. Does this sound rather daunting? Well, the best thing about it all is that there's plenty of room for error. Don't get the idea that everything rests on the next piece of chocolate you are (or are not?) going to eat! If you just get ever so slightly better at redesigning these connections, you'll do fine. Being able to do this in an imperfect way is something we'll look at in our next chapter.

This chapter is simply in order to understand what's actually happening. Then, you're not blindly following orders, following directions in this book just because I've told you to. You're using the principles because you understand them, because you know what you're doing.

We have been looking at the ways in which the brain changes, physically, by the ways in which you think. This is useful for two reasons. One, to understand that our familiar thoughts and actions are physically etched into our brains, and that's why we tend to get stuck in ruts. They really are like ruts or grooves, and it takes some effort to get out of them. The second thing is that this isn't permanent; these grooves can be changed with a little persistence. So you can accept the reality that these familiar patterns are there, and at the same time begin to make choices to do things differently, in the knowledge that in time and with practice things will get easier. They'll get easier because you'll be creating a new brain.

WHAT YOU CAN DO

- *Don't avoid the situations in which you tend to overeat.* They are not problems, but opportunities for you to make genuine changes. You don't need to make changes all at once. Take your time. See what it is that you really do want to change and be clear about why you want to change it. In time you'll probably want to develop new habits, hobbies and routines, but you do this having first made peace with your addictive desire to eat. Then, when you fall back into your old ways – and who doesn't every now and again? – you don't have to fall back into a binge as well.

- *Be willing to be repetitive.* The patterns in brain activation do change, but not instantaneously. It pays to be patient. Remember how many years you have been overeating. Is it realistic to expect that your memory of this will vanish like magic?

■ *Pay attention* to what you're doing when you expose yourself to the feelings of temptation. In general, things don't change by ignoring them. The more you actively attend to this process, the better results you get.

■ *Put words to what you are doing* by deliberately telling yourself, 'I am feeling an addictive desire to eat' and 'I have a choice about what I do.' Naming things, using words, is part of the process of linking up connections in the brain. It's deceptively simple, but getting into the habit of identifying and naming your addictive desire to overeat is a huge step forward.

■ *Replacing the eating connection with something else* isn't necessary and can actually mask the process, making it less effective. Diet colas are a common, unhelpful and unhealthy substitution for addictive overeating. The most common replacement, though, may be smoking cigarettes. When you smoke, of course, you are creating and strengthening brain connections with smoking. To make matters worse, whenever you try to stop smoking, the old associations with food return. If you are already a smoker, my book *Quitting smoking: The Lazy Person's Guide* will help you to stop. This will be your crucial, first step in taking real control of overeating.

■ Ask yourself the three questions:
'Am I choosing?'
'What's my motivation?'
'How am I responding to temptation?'

If you are unsure of what they mean or what to do about the answers, review the relevant chapters.

Iris's Story

The course raised a lot of awareness and I think the key lesson that remains is awareness of addiction. If you have a situation where you overeat and you remove the overeating from the situation, you create a vacuum. I had always been aware of that, but I had never known what to do about it. Whatever I did – got busy, exercised, socialised – the vacuum was always there. Now for the first time I have a name for it: it's my addictive desire to eat. That's been the big revelation for me, because naming it like that has stripped away all the extra bits and pieces I added to it and attributed to it. It used to mean I was incomplete, immature and somehow different from everybody else. At least, that's what I made it mean, but I can easily see now that it's just a memory of something I used to do. That realisation has changed so much for me and continues to do so.

I had been pregnant while I did the course and I wanted to do the best for my children and do the best for me. Even though I was enormous, it was because I was carrying twins and not because I had been pigging out! The course reinforced my healthy attitude. Without it I would have used pregnancy as an excuse to overeat, because nobody would know the difference. But I was aware whenever I ate: was it hunger and why was I eating this? I'm more aware of the excuses I would give myself and I realised that pregnancy was a wonderful excuse: 'I'm eating for three!'

CHAPTER 5

GIVE YOURSELF A BREAK

Chapters 1, 2 and 3 outline how to develop the most effective frame of mind to take control of overeating. With this way of thinking you'll have control at your fingertips, instead of chocolate and cake crumbs. Mostly you'll make progress through persistence, and through recognising the truth of your answers to the three questions.

However, there are some ways of thinking that you may bring to this process which can be obstacles that block your progress. When you understand what they are you'll be able to notice and overcome them. Then you continue unhampered, working towards developing more control over food. These obstacles are guilt, fear and perfectionism. You might encounter one of them as a problem, or two of them, or all three. Often they go hand in hand, so you might need to deal with each one to some extent. They aren't problems for everybody, however, so it could be that this chapter isn't so relevant to you.

Guilt

Guilt can be a valuable emotion so long as it doesn't last too long, dragging you down into chronic self-hatred. A certain amount of guilt is a valuable response to overeating because it lets you know you're doing something self-destructive. If you wrecked the health of somebody else, or if you kept lying or breaking your word to somebody else, you would expect to feel guilty about that, wouldn't you? Behaving in that way means that a certain amount of guilt is appropriate. It's telling you something, and all you need to do is to listen and see how you want to respond to what it's saying.

If you find yourself unable to respond to a reasonable sense of guilt, this could be a sign that you aren't really choosing. If this is the case, spend more time with Chapter 1. Take responsibility by choosing the consequences, which include guilt, along with the food.

Guilt becomes a serious obstacle when it's chronic. Then you feel guilty most of the time, possibly about pretty much everything, but especially about your eating and about how your body looks. Unrelenting guilt blocks your progress because it keeps you stuck in lower self-esteem. It takes some effort to change this, because you start out with little or no confidence in yourself.

This kind of self-hatred is often strongest when it's directed at body size, keeping you locked into weight loss as the main reason you want to eat less. For periods of time you may motivate yourself to improve your eating in an attempt to lose weight. Maybe you lose a bit and maybe you don't, but it's a slow process; your self-hatred is still there anyway, so it's easy for your motivation to fade. Then, it's often a case of, 'What the heck, I'm fat anyway, so why not go ahead and eat anything I want?' Either way, your choices about eating are all about how you look.

The reason appearance matters to you so much is because it's the aspect of the problem that everybody else can see and make their judgments about. But your harshest judge is you, and this is what keeps you from making real and lasting changes.

You change things by addressing the cause of the problem rather than the effect. Then you recognise that extra weight is just one of the effects created by your overeating and that there are many others. Mostly, those other effects have an impact on you and you alone, so starting to care more about yourself is the switch that makes the difference.

At first, it may feel as if you are pretending to care about yourself. It may not seem genuine, because it's new and different. It's a 'new you'. That's where you start out – with lower self-esteem.

With lower self-esteem, overeating may be a way to punish yourself. You overeat in a self-destructive way, knowing full well you'll regret it later on. You don't like yourself, so you have little interest in being kind to yourself. You are turned against yourself, and this is what keeps you helpless, anxious and even depressed. You don't think you're worth anything better than this, so there's little reason to change. And the overeating generates more guilt and lowers your self-esteem even more.

This toxic guilt can become a way of life, and overeating isn't necessarily the only aspect of your life it touches, although eating and weight may be central. The vicious circle is: 'I'm fat and worthless so I might as well eat more, so I overeat and then I get fatter and feel even more guilty, which proves I'm worthless, so I might as well eat some more ...'

If you recognise yourself here, you could be one of those extremely capable people who cover up their self-loathing with an over-committed, people-pleasing lifestyle. You rarely take time for yourself because you always put others first. If someone pays you a compliment, you find some way to invalidate it. If someone steps on your foot, you're the one who apologises. You find it tough to say 'no', and maybe you allow yourself to be walked over like a doormat. You rarely think of yourself, only of others. The chances are you've even been reading this book with someone else in mind.

Of course it's not a bad thing to look after people, and certainly at many times to put others first. It's a question of striking a balance. If you never prioritise your own needs, then that balance is not in your own best interests. It may not even be in the best interests of the people you are 'helping'.

If this is even close to your style, see if you use guilt as a stick to beat yourself with. Maybe you think that if you feel bad enough, you won't binge again. You may fear that if you eased up on the guilt and forgave yourself a bit, you'd never stop eating. But it absolutely doesn't work that way – and you know it doesn't, don't you?

Forgiving yourself doesn't make you apathetic. Having some compassion for yourself doesn't mean you then never want to change. In fact the reverse is true. If you wanted a child to develop in some way, to face his fears and try something new and challenging, you know instinctively that encouragement, recognition, patience and love are what will support him most. It's the same with you!

The antidote to exaggerated guilt is forgiveness. Forgiveness is a choice you can make by getting in touch with the spirit in you, who exists quite apart from anything you do and anything you happen to look like. Forgiveness is about claiming your worth, and you are the only one who can do that.

Fear

Fear comes in many varieties. Some *fear of failure* is probably inevitable, but for many it can seem not so much a fear as a certainty. Many people get so used to being out of control with eating that they have long ago resigned themselves to the way things are, giving up all possibility of real change.

They may at times go through some half-hearted motions of trying, in a sort of dreamy state of 'I really should do something about this.' Their deep resignation, though, means they won't put any real effort into it. If they really went for it and failed yet again, it would be so disappointing it's not worth the risk. So they make petty attempts at some superficial changes, fail (of course!) and resign themselves once again to the out-of-control norm. Usually something else gets blamed in this process, at least partly. So it becomes a case of, 'I would have stuck to it ... but my family ... but my job ... but my love of food got in the way.' This is how the fear of failure actually creates failure! It's a self-fulfilling prophecy.

Recognising this fear is a good place to start, so it's helpful to admit that you are afraid you'll fail. This, of course, requires some courage because you're acting in the face of fear, not in its absence. This is good, and you want to set your sights high enough so that some of your fear of failure appears. Aim high, but not purely in terms of weight loss. Chapter 7 may help you to find some other targets. Then, you get involved, putting as much effort and time and energy and attention into it as you can, even in the face of your conviction that it will never work. And guess what will happen then? You'll fail!

Let me explain. You see, there's failure and there's failure, and a certain amount of failure is absolutely inevitable. Not only is it to be expected, but it can even be valued as part of a learning process. Perhaps you've heard before that failure is part of learning. I was delighted when I found out that this idea was made famous by Thomas Edison. Often regarded as the greatest inventor ever, Edison was the first to record sound, he invented the electric light bulb still in use to this day, and in all took out over 1,000 patents for his inventions. By any measure he would be thought of as successful, at least in this area of his life.

Throughout it all, he regarded failure as an inevitable part of the process. I can just imagine him saying to himself, 'Well, that's another way not to make a light bulb ... and that's another way ... ' And so on until he got it right and the light bulb worked. I want to suggest to you that his positive relationship with failure was the major key to his success. If he had let his failures compromise his motivation and effort, he wouldn't have got there in the end.

To Edison, failure simply meant that there was something to learn, and it can mean that to you too. So any time you fail, either you give up trying or you look to see what there is for you to learn. It's not that failure is something to fear; it's how you respond to failure that determines your success in the long term.

Which brings us to *fear of success*, which can be just as much of an obstacle if you have low self-esteem. This is because not only will you expect to fail, but it will seem familiar, comfortable and safe. Success at anything at all can be frightening, and some people fear they will change too much and in ways they don't like. Lower self-esteem means that some otherwise very successful people make sure they sabotage themselves at least in one significant way, and often this is with eating.

Cope with this fear by taking things as they come, reminding yourself that you always have the freedom to return to overeating. It's always up to you, and if you don't like being in control of what you eat and all that this means, you don't have to stick with it! However, if your self-esteem remains low, it's likely you'll find some way to sabotage yourself. This is less likely to be a deliberate decision, but more of an inability to make changes that stick.

What makes the biggest difference here is in moving your motivation away from appearance and towards health. Wanting to look good reinforces low self-esteem. Wanting the best of health reinforces high self-esteem. You may well think that both are involved in your choices about food, but usually one type of motivation dominates.

Prioritise health, and as your self-esteem improves, your tendency to self-sabotage lessens. Higher self-esteem means you become less self-conscious and less sensitive to criticism, you feel more at ease and more at peace with yourself, more creative, productive and enthusiastic about life in general. In other words, you discover in time that there's not really too much to fear.

Fear of natural hunger, even of the slightest hint of it, often develops as a result of years of dieting. Following a diet is almost guaranteed to create a state of deprivation, so whenever natural hunger surfaces, it's met with anxiety and even panic at the thought of not being allowed to satisfy it. If this is a problem for you, you are probably aware that you overeat, even if it's just at meals, so that you can be sure you won't feel hungry before you can eat again. To some extent this makes sense, but it's very much a matter of degree. If you fear hunger so much that you never feel it at all, you'll find it tough to eat less even though you know you're eating far too much.

As with any fear, the way to overcome it is by facing it. Make sure some food is always available so that you absolutely know you are choosing whether or not you let yourself get hungry and for how long you feel it. If keeping your favourite treats with you means you can't stop thinking about them, keep food with you that's nourishing but not quite so attractive and compelling. Then, gradually allow yourself to move towards feeling your natural hunger. You don't need to skip meals in order to do this, but simply to eat less at your meals and perhaps to have fewer snacks in between.

Natural hunger isn't a bad thing. It's a signal to eat something soon, but it's perfectly normal and natural to feel it sometimes and it's not completely unpleasant. (If it's physically painful, it would be wise to see a doctor about that.) As much as you can, notice the difference between natural hunger and your addictive desire to eat. This can take time, and as we've already seen it's not completely reliable, but it can be valuable to know natural hunger and allow yourself to feel it at times.

As well as fearing natural hunger, you might also fear your addictive desire as well. Many overeaters *fear the addictive desire to eat* because it seems to overwhelm them and force them to eat addictively, despite their best efforts. This means they fight it and find it difficult to accept. As we saw in Chapter 3, when you fight it, it fights back, so the more you want it to go away, the more it's going to be there and the more it will seem to be a problem.

You will be able to overcome this fear if you remember this: your feeling of desire, uncomfortable as it is, doesn't make you eat. You eat because you want the feeling of desire to go away. Whenever you eat addictively, the addictive desire is satisfied at some point and then it's gone, at least for a while. You feel 'normal' again, but you've just gone through another binge.

By letting yourself accept your feeling of desire, you gain the ability to be in control. While you feel this desire, you are not overeating as a direct result. This is why it's so helpful to make the desire your friend instead of your enemy. If you're afraid of the dark you turn on a light, so shine a light on your addictive desire to eat and take a good look at it. When you do you'll see there are no monsters there, just an uncomfortable feeling of desire which will pass in time.

Perfectionism

Perfectionism is something you're sure to know you have if you have it. It's usually a habitual way of thinking about almost everything, certainly more than just about food. It shows up in those niggling thoughts that no matter what you achieve, you should have done better. With food, you are either absolutely in control of your eating with not a bite out of place, or you eat in a way that's completely indulgent with no real attempt to take any control at all. For a perfectionist, it's all or it's nothing.

Perfectionism makes it almost impossible to stay motivated, because any time any one thing is out of place, it's all completely invalidated. If it's not 100 per cent perfect, it's 100 per cent rubbish. Perfectionists zero in on the one thing that's wrong, and that one thing becomes everything. It becomes the evidence that you're not good enough and maybe never will be.

Many perfectionists tie eating 'perfectly' together with living 'perfectly'. For periods of time their eating is in a healthy and in-control phase, and their home is tidy and clean, the bed gets made every day, clothes get picked up and put away and the cat gets fed. Some people will tie in trips to the gym or abstaining from alcohol. Then, one thing goes wrong and it all goes wrong.

For many perfectionists, there's something hugely enjoyable about the 'perfect' phase. It generates a powerful 'high', a sense of exhilaration and energy that's hugely attractive. There's also a downside, though, and that can be an almost constant anxiety that it won't last.

And of course it doesn't last and it never will. It's a very tall order for anyone to stay in control of addictive eating perfectly. In the first place, it's impossible to define 'perfect eating'. The very idea conjures up silly questions such as, 'How many peas do I need for optimum health?' Obviously we can only make our best, educated guesses at what we need to eat each day. For the same reason, a definition of addictive overeating can only be approximate. It's only possible to say whether or not you eat addictively in terms of degree: 'a great deal' or 'not very much' or somewhere in between.

Aim for success in terms of degrees or percentages. Eliminate absolute success and you eliminate absolute failure at the same time. Get a picture of all the overeating you do when you're in your out-of-control phase, and call that 100 per cent addictive eating for you. If you then ate 10 or 20 per cent of that, that would be a pretty good result, wouldn't it? That's what you want to aim for. Then you can say, for example, 'I'm successfully in control of my eating about 80 per cent of the time.' Which is a lot better than nothing! Then you can acknowledge your successes, so then you can stay motivated.

If you think perfection is a reasonable goal, no matter what you accomplish, you will focus on the one thing 'wrong' and cancel out everything else. The 'perfect' phase looks like success, but it comes at a cost when the out-of-control phase kicks in as soon as something is out of place. Simply stop aiming for perfection. You don't need it in order to succeed.

It's not perfection that leads you to succeed in the long term. It's gaining an acceptance of your addictive desire to eat. When you have achieved that to a significant extent, then, even when you do eat addictively, you can easily get back into control by choosing to accept your feeling of desire.

WHAT YOU CAN DO

- *When you forgive yourself* for the overeating you've done, follow it up with an action to back it up. Make one choice to nurture yourself that's a little bit of a challenge. For example, if you often don't drink enough water, you might drink a glass or two as this symbolic act of forgiveness and self-nurturing. Or you might eat some fruit or choose to accept an addictive desire to eat something sugary. Eating something healthy can be every bit as positive a move in the right direction as not eating something that undermines your health.

- *Self-hatred* in the context we're looking at here is usually hatred of physical appearance. Whenever you think that you hate yourself, it's your body that you hate most, isn't it? The best place to start with this is to remember that you aren't just a body, but also a mind and spirit. When you can really appreciate your non-physical aspects, you'll be more able to honour your physical self as well by eating in a healthier way. Love your spirit first, and allow that love to seep into your mind. Then choices will follow more naturally that will develop a body to reflect that self-love.

■ *Visualise success* if you can, but don't worry if this is difficult for you to do. It's not essential to your success. Not only is it not essential, but very often an image of success is nothing more than an image of weight loss, and maybe a bit of an unrealistic one at that. If you visualise success at all, visualise yourself accepting your feelings of desire, willingly and without resistance. Once you've done that, you will be succeeding.

■ *Identify your fears* by completing the sentence: 'What I fear most about taking control of my overeating is ...' If you write them down, you'll be able to take them one by one and think about how real they are.

■ *Let go of black-and-white, all-or-none thinking.* Think instead in terms of shades of grey, or percentages. Aim for 80 per cent or whatever percentage seems to work for you. If that's too high, aim for 50 per cent and keep looking for ways to improve on that.

■ *Be willing to give up the high of perfection.* Whenever you're in one of your 'perfect' phases, deliberately eat in a way that's imperfect. Mess it up, here and there. You'll lose the thrill of perfection, but you'll also lose those plunges into the nightmare out-of-control eating when it all falls apart.

■ *What percentage of success* did you have with your eating today? Acknowledge one thing you did or didn't eat that you are pleased about.

Maggie's Story

There have been many benefits I've received from doing Gillian's course, but there's one that surprised me and this one has been a real joy. The reason it surprised me is because I had become so accustomed to the constant complaining in my head, a sort of whining to myself in the background or sometimes in the foreground of my thoughts, but never going away for very long. I was continually moaning to myself about what I ate and how I looked and how it wasn't at all like I wanted it to be. It was like going through life with someone whispering in your ear, 'You're a failure,' every minute of every day. It was only when I noticed it had gone that I realised it had been there, if you know what I mean. I don't think it's gone completely, I should say, but it's quite different now.

I did not like the idea of eating being an addiction, so that took some getting used to. It seemed much too judgmental and harsh. But it did give me a way to get out of this mental whining that things are not as you want them. It comes down to that fact that you can't continue to justify overeating and stop overeating at the same time. It sounds so obvious now that I'm writing this down, but that's what you really want, isn't it? You want the best of both worlds: overeating and no consequences. So the thing for me was to ask myself if this really was the way I wanted to live and if I was likely to get the consequences I'd want to live with later on.

The thing I find most helpful is planning your meal before you start eating, and I always do this with my evening meal. I have a little conversation with myself, checking if this really is what I want to eat and how much. I'm clear about it before I start eating and then I can be clear about it when I've stopped, because I always want to go on after I've finished. So then I think, that's what the addiction wants to eat: it's not what I want.

CHAPTER 6

CHOOSE YOUR REASONS

We're going to do some more troubleshooting in this chapter. I'll assume you've grasped the three questions, you're using them, you find they work well and you have been able to make some good changes in your eating. But there are still too many times when you go ahead and satisfy your addictive desire without thinking too clearly. So here's another aspect to the whole problem, an aspect which will enable you to control even these more difficult moments of desire. Often it's not that your desire for food is so intense and unacceptable: it's just that you've got a brilliant justification for satisfying it.

To start with, become aware of all the ways in which you justify satisfying your addictive desire. If you pay attention, you'll notice this justification just as you are about to eat, when you make your decision to go ahead and eat something in an addictive way. You might notice more than one justification at a time, and you probably use only a few over and over again. These few are your favourites: convincing, reasonable standbys you can always count on to get the food into your mouth.

Your justification might be that you'll enjoy it and you deserve it. It might be that this is just how you are, someone with no willpower who eats everything in sight. It might be that just one little bite won't make any difference. It's amazing how much you can eat with this one!

It's important to zero in on that moment of desire when you're about to eat addictively and to listen to what you're telling yourself at the time. There are other kinds of justifications people get attached to, and they are quite different. For example, people who say they are fat because it helps them hide from the world, or because their metabolism is slow, or so they can be less threatening to people. That's not what I'm talking about here. That is a way to try to make sense of overeating and weight, afterwards. These are unlikely to be the kinds of things you say to yourself when you're about to eat, when you justify satisfying your addictive desire. It's not likely that you think, 'I'm going to eat this box of donuts so that I can be less threatening to people.'

It's good to know your justifications, because it's only when you've got them identified that you can take a good look at them. Then you can choose either to use them or to throw them out. You get into the habit of noticing whenever you're thinking along the lines of 'I fancy some ice cream', for example, and then the most appropriate justification at the time gets you to satisfy that desire.

You may have found already that many justifications simply fall away when you realise that all you're really doing is satisfying an addictive desire. Many more fall away when you take on board that it's always your choice. When you are operating in that state of deprivation, you attach yourself very strongly to your justifications. They become crucial because they provide you with the freedom to overeat that you so desperately need. So your justifications mean a lot more to you when you aren't really choosing. For example, 'I'm not allowed to eat wheat, but I was hungry and that was all there was in the house' looks completely reasonable, logical and convincing. It might be reasonable once, but not over and over again. Moving into a state of choice means realising wheat can be freely chosen, along with the consequences. Then, the justification loses its significance.

Something that can be tricky about justifications is that they pop up tailor-made for more unusual situations, especially one you're experiencing for the first time since taking control. As we saw in Chapter 4, there's usually a stronger sense of desire when you encounter something for the first time since you took more control of your eating. This is assuming, of course, that it's a situation in which you would have eaten addictively in the past. Suddenly, there's that particular memory and along with it a justification completely suited to that circumstance. The desire may be minor, but the justification is a nifty one you haven't met and dealt with before.

Often, a number of things converge. There's an intensity of feeling that you're encountering for the first time since working with this approach, so there's a brain connection that has yet to weaken. Plus, an extremely good justification, one so good nobody would blame you if you overate, especially yourself. Plus a circumstance in which you would have overeaten anyway, such as a visit to your parents or a wedding.

It really is tough to stay so aware and on top of this all the time, so you may well miss some of them and overeat. You may not mind too much if it's just now and again. But if it's happening so often it gets to be a problem, try spotting the justification you keep using and see what you can do about it. When you're too attached to your justifications too much of the time, it will be tough to accept the feeling of desire.

Perhaps the most common and challenging justification is to comfort yourself when you're feeling low. If this is one you're ready to break through, understand first that there are many variations on this justification, each one slightly different.

As we've already seen, your addictive desire is very likely to be connected to emotions, in exactly the same way that it's associated with a routine such as taking a coffee break, or a situation such as taking a long car journey. If you eat any time you experience a particular feeling, whether it's subtle or strong, then you'll experience a desire to eat whenever that feeling comes along, be it anger, frustration, rejection, loneliness, sadness or whatever. You weaken the connection when you're feeling the emotion and the addictive desire to eat, and you choose not to reinforce that connection.

For some people, though, 'comfort eating' isn't so much that you're overwhelmed by feelings at the time, but that traumatic and deeply upsetting events happened in your past. The trauma may have passed long ago, but it gets referred to in your thoughts, ever so briefly, and this becomes a favourite justification: 'Such-and-such happened to me in the past, so I'm going to go ahead and eat.' You probably call that comfort eating; you have these bad memories and so you comfort yourself with food. That sounds reasonable, doesn't it? Yes it does, but another way to explain it is that you have an addictive desire to eat, and you habitually justify satisfying it by remembering these events. It's like having a free pass to all the eating you ever want to do.

You may need to explore these painful memories, perhaps with the support of a therapist, a personal development programme or a good self-help book, and it's entirely possible that you could benefit from that. But if you have already done that and you are still overeating, it's just because you haven't taken the next step. The next step is to refuse to use this justification any more and to start making choices to accept your addictive desire. You decide that, yes, these things happened to you in the past, but you don't want to continue to use them to justify overeating.

It's a common idea that those who overeat carry some deep wound that needs to be healed, but that isn't always the case. Sometimes people start to overeat because of some difficulty in their lives, but when the difficulty has passed the addictive relationship with food persists, simply because the addictive desire continues to be fed and reinforced.

Sometimes it isn't a particular tragedy that leads you to overeat, but an ongoing sense of imbalance in your life, a sense of things being not as they should be. It may be true that when life is in balance, you are more in control with food and find it easy to eat in the least addictive way. But all this really means is that you have more of an addictive desire to eat when you're out of balance. You still have the option of accepting your addictive desire, even when nothing else seems to be going right. Especially in these times, it can seem like a miracle not to overeat, and this can be the one thing you can find delight in at that time. There are a great many things in life that you have absolutely no control over and no choice about, but at least your eating doesn't have to be one of them.

Then, of course, there are the more dramatic events in your life that stir up strong feelings in the present, and you have some of the strongest justifications of all. You think, 'Given that this is going on in my life, I wouldn't really expect myself to stay in control of my eating; nobody would, in these circumstances.' So, more comfort eating: 'I want it, I need it, I deserve it and I'm going to have it.'

At these times passions can seem to override reason, making any rational approach utterly useless. It's true that emotions can get the better of us at times – but it's not inevitable. I want to suggest that there are times you have strong feelings but don't act on them. This is really the same as those people who sober up after alcohol or drug addiction. It's not that these people no longer feel miserable sometimes: it's that they find ways to deal with those feelings other than the medication of drug abuse.

Comforting yourself with food when you're completely distraught seems reasonable, but ask yourself how often that really happens, and how distraught you actually need to be in order to justify overeating. Comfort eating may help you with the hurt, but doesn't it also create its own kind of hurt? Maybe it's time to weigh these up and choose which is going to hurt the least in the long term.

For some people comfort eating isn't so much because of the difficulty of the feelings, but more that there's an unrealistic expectation that you should never have these feelings. Things start to go wrong not because you feel low, but because you think you shouldn't ever feel this way. In fact, these feelings are part of life, and I bet you know that. You may know, for example, that quite often people who are prescribed anti-depressants don't like to take them because they make them feel flat and somewhat emotionless. Feelings are what keep us feeling (!) alive.

Not only that, but understanding persistent feelings can be your best guide to all kinds of decision making. Feelings are trying to tell you something. They are a sign that either something needs to change in your life because it's causing you distress, or that you need to look at changing your reaction to whatever is happening. Maybe a bit of both. Obviously there's usually quite a learning process there in figuring out which is which; what you want to change and what you want to handle in a new way. But overeating certainly doesn't help you with any of it.

Comfort eating is also the way people describe overeating in response to stress. If this is your biggest justification, be aware that addictive overeating makes stress much worse, not better. Here are the facts about stress and food.

First, the high-GI carbohydrate foods actually increase your stress level by stimulating the release of the stress hormone, cortisol. They are very commonly overeaten in times of stress, but the truth is the less you eat them, the less stressed you'll feel. Second, stress creates muscle tension in readiness for the 'fight or flight' response. Tense muscles use up more vitamins and minerals, so you actually need more nutrient-dense food (in particular fruits and vegetables) than when you're relaxed. Third, the stress 'fight or flight' mechanism shuts down digestive processes, because digestion is a low priority in the whole scheme of things when you're under attack. This is why it's much better to eat more simple, natural food and not to overeat. A fourth reason to eat more wisely in times of stress is that stress weakens the immune system.

When you feel stressed and you overeat, all you accomplish is to use feeling stressed as a way to justify satisfying your addictive desire. In doing so you reinforce the association between stress and overeating, and set yourself up for more stress and more overeating.

Another way to look at the justifications is to think of them as the conditions you place on successfully taking control of addictive eating. For example, you might think along the lines of, 'If only I was happier and felt more secure, I'd stop eating so much junk food,' or 'If only I wasn't so busy looking after my children ... ' or 'If only I had more money ... '

You break through these by taking responsibility, by recognising that you're the one who created the overeating in the first place, that you're the one who chose it. When you blame other people and situations and circumstances, this disempowers you because you make yourself a victim of circumstance. When you say 'I did it' you get the possibility of changing it, because it's all in your hands. If you're the one who did it, then you're the one who can do it differently. If you blame your upbringing, your genes, your family or your job, then there's not much you can do about it.

You see, if it's really worth it to you, you won't follow through on the addictive desire even when you've got the best excuse in the world. If it's worth it to you. This is exactly where the more superficial motivation tends to fall apart. That's why it's better to connect with motivation that's more empowering and more immediate than weight loss, to connect with the amazing quality of life you get as a result of taking control of your eating. Then you can say, 'I either have this miserable situation in my life and I overeat, or I have this miserable situation in my life and I don't overeat.'

And really, what's the difference? The illusion is that your overeating helps you cope with the situation, but your biggest breakthroughs occur when you discover that if anything, the reverse is true. Staying in control of your overeating brings you more confidence and higher self-esteem, and this will support you through tough times far more than overeating ever can. The key here is to be willing to accept the uncomfortable feeling of desire, even when everything else is going badly.

It has often been said that when it comes to overeating, it's not *what* you eat, it's *why* you eat that's the key. I would agree with that, but suggest a different answer to the 'why' than is usually offered. Usually, what's offered is a justification. Why you overeat, for example, is because you're sad. But you also overeat when you're happy, when you're celebrating, when you're lonely, when you're busy and when you're bored. The truth is you overeat in lots of different circumstances.

The only consistent answer to the question of 'why' is because you have an addictive desire to eat, which you satisfy. That's the bottom-line answer. Anything else is a justification for satisfying the addictive desire. The justification can be exposed as a flimsy excuse, but the addictive desire remains until it has faded. It fades when it's accepted and no longer reinforced.

The greatest benefit in understanding this is that you don't need to wait until the addictive desire has disappeared before you start to make real changes. Many people try to fix the justification – the sadness, for example – in the hope that their addictive desire will go with it. Sometimes this way seems to work, mostly because the justification has gone. But difficult feelings will always be a part of our lives. For most of us, the moments are rare when we feel perfectly balanced, at peace with the world and only interested in a small salad for lunch.

WHAT YOU CAN DO

■ *Notice the justification* you give yourself next time you overeat. If you find it difficult to identify the justification, delay satisfying your addictive desire for a while and it will probably become clearer and more urgent. Just like somebody trying to attract your attention.

■ *Discover your favourite justifications* by completing the sentences, 'If only ... then I'd be able to take control of my overeating' and 'I overeat because ...'

■ *Coping with your addictive desire to eat* often takes place in the supermarket, when you walk down the aisles and hear your favourite snacks calling out to you. If you buy addictive foods in the shops, obviously you are likely to eat them. If you don't buy them, you won't. If you buy them for others but often end up eating them yourself, be honest with yourself about that – and choose what you really want to do.

■ *If you often buy addictive food for others*, you might want to ask yourself why you are doing that in the first place. Do you really want to perpetuate this problem in your own immediate community, or start to solve it? See if you can find healthier options to offer your family and friends. Healthier options usually don't have that addictive 'kick' to them, so they aren't as attractive and compelling.

■ *If lack of money* is your favourite justification for eating manufactured food, please understand that in terms of nutrition (rather than addiction) you are much better off eating real food. Processing, packaging, advertising and marketing all cost a great deal of money, so that's what you're really paying for. People spend their working lives creating slogans such as '95 per cent fat-free' for something that's mostly sugar, and 'made with olive oil' for a sauce that's mostly vegetable oil. Who pays their wages? You?

■ *You've started, so why not continue?* If what you've read of this book so far has made sense to you but you haven't put it into practice yet, look to see how you are justifying that. Too busy? Doesn't feel right? Keep forgetting about it? It's entirely possible that the best time to get more involved is sooner rather than later. Your resistance is unlikely to go away, so if you leave this book on a shelf it could mean it will stay there for a very long time.

Emily's Story

I've been studying food as medicine for close to 20 years. All that time ago I discovered macrobiotics and it was a revelation to me that you could feel so much better by what you ate, and that it could make such a difference. That whole idea was new to me. I had been ill with a thyroid problem and it was important for me to get my health back, so when I learned about macrobiotics it was really out of need. I stuck with it religiously for a year and then I just got bored with it. I wanted to eat chocolate and cheeses and desserts and all those kinds of things.

I knew how to eat for optimum health and yet I would play games. I would know that if I ate high-fat food, like chocolates and cheeses and chips, I'll feel sluggish and sleepy and guilty. I would have them on hand to offer to friends who visit and then, when things got hectic and especially when I found myself in a relationship that taxed me emotionally, I would find myself bingeing, rationalising madly all the while.

I've found that the part about choice and choosing was like a life net for me. Now, I can be in the choosing mode, and not just about food. If I remind myself that I can have this treat, anytime I want it, it gives me power. It's amazing to me how much power there is in that!

If it weren't for being in the choosing mode I'd have had a ghastly sticky-bun at my gym this morning. There was a special workout event scheduled today and they provided treats afterwards, including bagels and cream cheese, muffins and sticky-buns, coffee, tea and a bit of fruit. Of course the fruit disappeared first, and the damn buns were glaringly left behind. I could have had several, as they'd just be thrown out. I considered bringing them home, to give away or put in the freezer for a special occasion. Ha! I left them there. Whew.

I think at some level all compulsive behaviours are connected; they are simply various forms of self-medication that are part of one big symptom – which is self-esteem. When you get a handle on other stuff it's easier to get your eating or your drinking under control, if you look it squarely in the face. When you're in denial, it's across the board and it's easier not to do laundry, not to exercise, not to pay the bills. It goes in cycles and as you get one thing together and rein one thing in, the other things tighten up. If you can stay right there at the centre, the more focused you become and the more you get done. Some people don't ever rein anything in: they just keep going. I used to think I would be one of them, but that's changing now.

CHAPTER 7

THE GOOD STUFF

Did you know that two of the best known names in the food industry – Kraft and Nabisco – are owned by the world's largest tobacco company, Philip Morris, the manufacturers of Marlboro cigarettes? Think about it. Do you think Philip Morris executives care about your health? Maybe you think that comparing cigarettes with Oreo cookies and Ritz crackers is stretching things a bit, but I'm wanting to make an important point. Don't trust the food industry with your life. Look at how much manufactured, processed food you consume, and if it's much more than a few bites here and there, you may be doing just that.

Our language makes it difficult to see, because we simply don't have ways to describe what's happened to the things we eat over the last couple of decades. Even the phrases 'junk food' and 'convenience food' include the word 'food'. They are not food, and far from being benign, these products actually do your body harm. They make you ill in much the same way as cigarettes make smokers ill.

How can I be so sure? Let's look at this another way. How would you like to stay younger for longer in your life? Of course nothing changes how fast the years go by, but how fast your body ages, that's very much up to you. Even if you're not so interested in living past 100, the quality of however many years you have left is at least partly determined by the quality of the food you eat. This, as much as anything else you can do, will determine the length of time you stay in good health, able to do what you want to do, have some independence and be free from pain and disease. It is completely realistic to expect to go through your old age feeling strong and in good health.

Advances in biomedical research over the past decade help us understand aging better than ever before and show us how we can extend and enhance the quality of our lives. This information provides you with the best motivation there is, because when you support your health you support your self-esteem. In this chapter you'll see how to do just that – but first a reminder.

Many people won't take on board information about health and nutrition, and the reason they resist it is because they think it means they won't be able to indulge themselves in their favourite 'naughty' treats any more. In other words, the feelings of deprivation, from thinking you aren't free to eat whatever you want, threaten to take over. Notice as you read this chapter if you are feeling as if you are being told you can't or mustn't eat processed food, or that you have to eat less of it. If you tend to think in this way, you're likely to reject the information.

Correct this way of thinking by reminding yourself that you are free to eat anything you want and as much as you want. You've always got choices, and that's where you need to start off, knowing you're free to do whatever you want. If reading this far has sent you running off for the Ritz cracker box, keep letting yourself know that you're allowed to eat them all, and you can go out and buy another box and eat all of that as well. And so on. What you don't have a choice about is which consequences follow from the choices you make. This chapter is about how you can know what it is you're choosing, so that you can make educated choices by choosing the consequences along with whatever you're eating.

You might also resist nutritional information because you find it too confusing and contradictory. It is true that it can be complicated, and the jury is still out on some of it, but here are three of the most important and well-established principles, as clear and concise as possible.

Cellular Health

When your cells are healthy, you are healthy. It makes sense, doesn't it? All the degenerative diseases have been shown to be strongly associated with cellular damage: heart disease, hardened arteries, high blood pressure, stroke, cancer, arthritis, adult-onset diabetes, Alzheimer's, Parkinson's, cataracts, and the list goes on.

Our cells become damaged through the excess production of unstable molecules called 'free radicals' and through damage to the cell membrane. Some amount of cell damage is inevitable, just as aging is inevitable, and the damage accumulates, so the older we get the more likely the effects will become serious problems.

However, it's very much in our hands as to how much and how fast the damage occurs. We can keep it to a minimum in two ways. One way is to avoid damaging the cells as much as possible. The other way is to eat the foods that neutralise the damage and heal the cells.

Cells become damaged faster by smoking, environmental pollution, x-ray and sun exposure, stress, excessive alcohol, excessive exercise – and through some of the things we eat. As far as our food is concerned, most of this damage occurs through consuming the most common kinds of fats. These are most of the common vegetable oils and especially the hydrogenated oils, also known as trans fats. They are to be found in manufactured foods (snack foods, biscuits, crackers, pasties, pies, cakes, margarines, etc.) and of course anything fried or baked with oil (chips, chicken, pizza, fish, etc). Other substances in foods which contribute to cellular damage are monosodium glutamate (MSG), artificial sweeteners, pesticides and herbicides.

The good news is that much of the damage is reversible. The antidotes are the antioxidants, vitamins, minerals, flavinoids and enzymes, all to be found in fresh fruits, vegetables, whole grains, nuts and seeds. The different colours of these foods – reds, yellows and greens – indicate different varieties of antioxidants, so eat a wide variety. The antioxidants do not work properly in isolation, but together as a team.

As some amount of cell damage occurs daily, these nutrients need to be replaced daily. The immediate benefit is to your immune system.

Fat Loss Or Muscle Loss

When you don't provide your body with the nutrition it needs you can lose weight, but the weight you lose is valuable lean muscle tissue rather than fat. This has the effect of aging your body. We all lose muscle as we get older, and by middle age you could have lost about 6½ pounds (3 kilograms). This rate of muscle loss usually increases in old age, but it's up to you how much and how fast that happens. There are very good reasons to maintain as much muscle as you can.

Muscle is metabolically active, so the more muscle you have

the faster you burn calories, even when you're asleep. A pound of muscle burns calories 20 times faster than a pound of fat, so the more muscle is lost, the slower your metabolism and the easier it is to gain even more fat. This is why crash dieters often find the fat piles back on as soon as they end the diet. As muscle is considerably heavier than fat, the weight loss achieved can seem impressive, but doesn't last and is disastrous for your health.

On the other hand, eating wisely and exercising even a moderate amount means more muscle gained and more fat lost. This way you could stay pretty much the same weight but look a lot slimmer. This way you are much more likely to maintain your improved shape in the long term.

And not only will you look better, but you'll be considerably healthier, as more muscle means you're much less likely to suffer from a number of other age-related problems. These include loss of bone density, which ends up as osteoporosis, and reduced blood sugar tolerance, which ends up as adult-onset diabetes. Muscles are 75 per cent water, so drinking the recommended 8 to 10 glasses a day will also contribute to muscle maintenance.

Blood Sugar Levels

This is the popular term for the imbalance in insulin production which we looked at briefly in Chapter 3 as a cause of false hunger. This imbalance is thought by many to have other implications, both on our ability to lose weight and on the state of our health.

Food that creates this imbalance is any carbohydrate with a high 'glycemic index' (GI). They are usually the most addictive foods and thus the most overeaten; most commonly sugar, all forms of potatoes and processed grains, including most commercial breads, cereals, cakes and biscuits. Our bodies respond to all of these as sugars, and are not designed to deal with them in any quantity. Not only do they upset blood sugar levels, but they also require the production of a vast number of hormones to cope with the imbalance.

Eating too many high-GI carbohydrates is associated with chronic low blood sugar (mood swings, headaches and dizziness), fatigue, adult-onset diabetes, high blood pressure and heart disease.

Occasional high-GI carbohydrates aren't so dangerous; the problem is that people eat too many of them too often. To lessen their effects, eat them less often, and when you do balance them with proteins and low-GI foods.

Well-modulated insulin levels result in: greater reduction of body fat, no false hunger, increased and sustained energy, increased mental alertness, and reduced high blood pressure and cholesterol. The best place to find lists of the glycemic ratings of carbohydrates is on the Internet. Do a word-search for 'glycemic index' and you will find lots of information. A couple of books on the subject are mentioned in the reading guide at the end of this book.

You don't need to be confused, because the basic formula is simple and very well established. For those of you who need to learn quite a bit in this area, I've listed a few good books at the end of this book. To put it all in as short a form as possible:

Eat a balanced and diverse diet, low in calories and high in nutrients. Include three servings of fruit and five of vegetables every day. Don't forget pulses and whole grains. Eat fish twice a week and red meat no more than once a week.

Eat a diet low in fat, especially saturated and trans fats, which are completely unnecessary and should be kept to an absolute minimum. Some kinds of fat are essential, especially omega 3 and omega 6, mostly found in nuts, seeds and oily fish such as mackerel, tuna, salmon and herring. More healthy fats are the monounsaturated fats, such as those found in olive oil, canola oil and avocados.

Food, of course, certainly isn't the only thing that affects aging and your health. Genes, levels of stress and activity, how optimistic or pessimistic you are, and the love and support you live with all play their part.

When it comes to genes, though, there's no need to be fatalistic, as your health is only partly determined by the genes you inherit. You may have inherited a genetic tendency for a particular disease, but it's poor nutrition that can activate your weakest genetic link. The only time it's too late to make changes is when you're dead. Assuming you're not dead, you can begin to improve your health and your chances of staying healthy by choosing to make changes in what you eat on a daily basis, and if you don't already exercise, by becoming more active.

Many people have developed the notion that there's no such thing as 'good' food and 'bad' food. It's all fine, they say, so long as you don't eat too much of any one thing. This is their way of protecting themselves against feeling deprived. Now you know better. See if your idea of a wide variety is in fact a wide variety of sugar, processed grains, fat and salt, all combined and packaged in different ways.

If you don't wake up to the difference between real food and

THE GOOD STUFF 97

anti-food, you'll find it tough to take control of overeating. When you take control, you choose food based on its being good for your body. It's important to enjoy it too, but enjoyment isn't the only consideration. When you eat in an addictive way, enjoyment is your top priority and nutrition barely counts. So choose which way you want to go, and choose the consequences you are willing to live with.

As an example of some of these consequences, studies conducted at hospitals have demonstrated the crucial role nutrition plays for patients undergoing surgery. In a general survey, as many as 60 per cent of those admitted were found to be malnourished to some degree, and this was strongly linked to more infections, pneumonia, problems with wound healing and even mortality rates after surgery.

A trend now appearing is that degenerative diseases usually associated with old age are increasingly showing up in younger people. Adult-onset diabetes is becoming more common in teenagers. Autopsies of teenagers killed in accidents show signs of heart disease. Angina has become an epidemic in the UK, showing up even in those in their 20s. Smoking is a major cause, but high fat diets and lack of exercise are also key factors. Nearly half of all sufferers are women.

All these are previously unheard of, and it is widely believed that more than anything else, they are due to poor nutrition.

WHAT YOU CAN DO

■ *Nutritional supplements* are a very good idea, especially for those who find it difficult to eat enough fresh fruit and vegetables every day. Make sure you use whole food supplements, as vitamin and mineral pills do not provide you with anything like the complete range of antioxidant vitamins, minerals, flavinoids, phytochemicals and enzymes. You'll find more information at the end of this book.

■ *Find out if you are you overweight* to the extent that it's a health risk or simply in a way that's unfashionable. You may need to consult a health professional because this depends on your level of fitness, your age and muscle mass as well as amount of fat. Your 'body mass index' is a very rough guide, and it is generally thought that a BMI of 24 and above is associated with a higher risk of serious illnesses such as heart disease, high blood pressure, osteoarthritis and adult-onset (type 2) diabetes.

■ *Find out if you are overweight* because you aren't active enough, rather than because you eat too much of the wrong things. Even if you eat exactly what you need and no more, it's difficult not to gain weight if you are inactive. And if you are already overweight, it's very difficult to lose the weight through eating less alone, without some exercise as well. Energetic walking is often considered the best, and the main value is that it builds muscle. It's a case of use it or lose it.

■ *When making choices* about what you eat, ask yourself if you are about to increase free radical damage or antioxidant production. Or find out if you are about to eat high-GI carbohydrates. This is a far better way to make choices than by thinking in terms of weight lost or gained. If you really care about your health you will lose weight (assuming you're overweight to start with), but you'll be achieving it in an empowering and sustainable way.

■ *When making choices, know that saturated and trans fats* are by far the worst for your health. Saturated fat is found in red meat, whole-fat dairy products and palm and coconut oils. Trans fats are found in hard margarines and many oils, but are largely hidden in commercial products such as potato crisps, biscuits, bread, cakes, pies and crackers. Look for hydrogenated oil on the labels, but even labels won't identify all the trans fats.

■ *When making choices, know that sugar drains nutrients* from the body, so think of sugar as the opposite of a vitamin pill. The single best thing you can do for your health may be to reduce your sugar intake. Your body regards refined carbohydrates as sugar, so white rice, refined cereals and breads have the same effects as table sugar and glucose. The best wheat bread to buy is 100 per cent stone ground.

■ *If chocolate is your thing,* have you ever thought about upgrading the quality of what you buy? Chocolate itself may even be beneficial, but not when relatively small amounts are mixed together with very poor quality fats and refined sugar, as is the case with most popular commercial bars and sweets. You could accept your addictive desire for the endless fixes of flavoured, sugary fat and save your money for more occasional, top-quality brands. Often, when you've developed a taste for the finer chocolates, the cheaper ones can become a lot less interesting.

■ Do you drink enough water? Thirst is probably an even less reliable body signal than hunger. At least 8 glasses of water are recommended every day, which few of us actually feel a need for. That's water, not just any liquid. Coffee, tea, alcohol and fizzy drinks not only don't count, but as they contain diuretics you'll need even more water if you drink them frequently. Our sense of thirst is known to diminish as we age and chronic dehydration is thought to be a factor in a wide range of common illnesses.

Ruby's Story

I'm an accountant, not a writer, so I hope this makes sense. I still want to lose weight, but these are the benefits I'm getting right now and I can hardly believe how thrilled and excited I am with them. Weight loss is great but it's certainly not the whole picture any more, nor even the biggest part of it.

Better skin condition
The idea of becoming a completely new person through the generation of healthy cells
No more frequent sore throats due to a weak immune system
Ability to breathe easily
Less risk of a heart attack
Less risk of varicose veins, which runs in my family
Risk of cancer is lower due to healthier cells

No more hair loss due to poor nutrition

Feel like a cat (all stretched and supple) when I wake up, instead of bloated

No more shame (that inability to look the shopkeeper in the eye when I buy sweets)

No more hiding what and how much I eat

No more roller coaster eating and the emotions attached to it

I can eat sweets if I want to, any time and any amount; they will still be there tomorrow and the diet doesn't start then

No more fear of going out with friends because it might ruin my diet

No more boring my friends with my weight problems and diet stories

I can stare down a cookie

I control food, it doesn't control me; the invisible monster really doesn't exist

No more waking up every morning in a state of fear and panic, wondering if I'm going to stick to my diet that day.

I noticed an interesting justification this morning. I woke up and decided that since it's my birthday, I'll have cookies and tea to celebrate. This was at 6 o'clock in the morning. Then I realised that I don't have to justify it! I decided it's fine, reached for the cookie jar and suddenly didn't feel like it. This is probably my first birthday ever that I am not stuffing my face with cake! There was a box of chocolates in the office the whole day. I decided to eat four, had them, enjoyed them, and the box never bothered me for the rest of the day.

CHAPTER 8

STAYING AHEAD OF THE GAME

Imagine you live in a world where some food will keep you healthy and some will make you ill, and everybody seems not to know which is which. Imagine that talented and creative people are paid good money to convince you to eat the food that will make you ill. Imagine that everyone you know eats it and pretends it's good for them. Imagine you live in a world where the best way to get though a day is with the least amount of physical effort. Imagine that children are taught that the best way to honour themselves is through impressing others; that the most important thing in life is to look good at any cost.

It doesn't matter if you don't have much of an imagination, because in one way or another you already live in this world. To better understand the impact our environment has on us, let's look at the many examples of people whose culture changed quite dramatically.

The best example may be the people of the Western Samoa Islands in the Pacific. A generation ago they were still fairly isolated from the rest of the world, living in more natural ways and eating food grown locally. The discovery of valuable natural resources created enormous wealth, and the islanders now have one of the highest per capita incomes in the world. They have also become the most obese nation in the world.

Their wealth has meant that they can now be much less active.

It has also attracted the Western food industry, so that the traditional diet of fish, vegetables and fruit has been replaced by manufactured, processed food. About three-quarters of their population have now become obese and one-third diabetic.

There are also examples of people who moved from one culture to another with similar results. In their traditional culture, the Japanese have the lowest rates of heart disease and are the longest-lived people in the world. Those who emigrate to America, though, become overweight and get heart disease just as much as other Americans. Similar comparisons have been made between Afro-Americans and their African relatives.

Another example can be found in the experience of a group of American Indians. The Pima Indians of Arizona lived and farmed on the land as their ancestors did, up until the 1980s when they were granted a casino concession and became extremely wealthy. They now live a comfortable American lifestyle, and eat a more American diet. They are now considered to be the fattest group of people in the United States.

Their wealth means the Pimas can afford the best hospitals – and they need them. Their excess weight has lead to hypertension, high blood pressure, bone, muscle and joint strains and many kinds of cancer. More than half of them have become diabetic.

For their genetic cousins, another group of Pimas who live in Mexico, diabetes and obesity are virtually unknown. Mexican Pimas spend much of their time in physical labour on the land, eating a diet high in vegetable fibre and low in fat.

These examples show clearly the impact of our modern culture, with its constant supply of attractive but toxic food, on weight and health. But this is not intended to leave you in a state of gloom and doom about being able to make changes without emigrating to the North Pole. First of all, it shows you that genes are not responsible for overeating, because genes don't change that fast. Second, it's less likely that unresolved emotional trauma is the main cause either. It's not likely that a more affluent culture made whole populations less capable of dealing with their emotions, or with deep emotional scars in need of healing. What makes much more sense is having easy access to enormous quantities and varieties of highly addictive but deadly food. These days, we are surrounded by it.

There was just one kind of potato crisp when I was a child in the 1950s. The only choice anyone had was whether or not to open up the little packet of salt and shake it over the crisps, or to eat them unsalted. Now there's usually a whole aisle in each supermarket devoted to different varieties. Lest we make the supermarkets the villains, let's remember that the only reason they are on sale is because people buy them. It's marketed to you, you buy it, it's hugely lucrative, so people manufacture and market more of it. You are an active link in that chain, not a victim of it. It's possible to walk down those aisles and not put that stuff in your trolley!

A good principle to remember is that if it's advertised and marketed, it's addictive. Anything addictive sells itself, which is why sugar, salt, processed grains and fat are included in these processed foods.

Not only has our culture accepted unhealthy food as the norm, but at the same time slimness has been promoted as the ideal, especially for women. Through advertising, movies, TV and the rest, the message is that if you're slim you're a good person and if you're overweight you don't count. Even when health issues are acknowledged, it's far more common to talk about a weight problem rather than an eating problem, keeping you focused on just one effect.

When you stay focused on weight it can be tough to stay motivated, because weight loss is so slow. Perhaps your first waking thought is the realisation of how overweight you still are, and this sense of failure before you've even begun can undermine any motivation you may have had. You think maybe you'll make it through another day in control, if you're lucky, but even if you do you'll still be overweight.

It makes a big difference to keep in mind those benefits which give you more immediate feedback. The more you can relate to them – feeling in control, taking care of yourself, self-respect, feeling more relaxed around food, feeling healthier, better digestion and sleep – the more you can stay motivated. It's not that weight ever becomes something that doesn't matter at all. Of course it matters, and will continue to matter to the vast majority of us. It's just that you include some other motivation, so that appearance isn't the only thing – and maybe not even the most important thing.

There's a paradox in this: keep letting go of wanting to lose weight and it will be much more likely to happen. Focus on healthier eating, and once you've lost the weight you'll have good reasons to stay with it, regardless of your size. You'll need those good reasons, because temptation will be there no matter what you weigh.

An addictive relationship with food isn't something that goes away, but it is something you can learn to deal with so that it becomes far less of a problem. Most people try to control their eating by trying to avoid temptation. If you do that, you never learn how to deal with your addictive desire to eat, so you're almost guaranteed to return to overeating. This doesn't mean you're a hopeless failure. It just means you haven't yet developed the skill of dealing with your addictive desire. Maybe you didn't know how to do that before you came across this book, but now you do: you allow yourself to feel it, accepting it because it's the way you stop eating so much.

A genuine feeling of free choice is essential, so keep reminding yourself you don't have to do any of this. You can keep overeating all your life. It's when you deny that freedom that you find yourself hoovering up everything in sight, always fearing this will be your last meal, or your last overindulgent meal. When food is forbidden you've absolutely *got to* eat it *now*, because this may be your last chance.

You turn this on its head by letting yourself know you can eat this food, whatever it is. You can have as much you want and you can come back tomorrow and have some more. This food, or something like it, is going to be available to you and you can have it every day, for breakfast, lunch and dinner and snacks in between. Just remember the complete picture of what you're choosing; the downside as well as the upside. Be honest about it if this is not at all good for your health.

Your success depends very much on what you're aiming for. If you're aiming for the perfect figure you could be looking for trouble, especially without a great deal of exercise. Very few people can maintain that ideal of slimness and at the same time have a truly healthy relationship with food. If, however, you aim for better health, more energy, improved fitness, greater self-esteem and a longer, healthier old age, then success is within everyone's grasp.

As much as you possibly can, buy your food in its original packaging, the one designed hundreds of generations ago. Follow nutritional advice and a reasonable exercise programme, and you will certainly get results. You can turn around any signs of ill health you already have. And if you are already in the best of health you can take preventative measures, being active rather than passive in maintaining your good health. Think holistically, in that wherever you start to make changes, results appear on each level of body, mind and spirit.

It makes sense to me that addictive behaviour is related to all three of these realms: physical, mental and spiritual. To say, as many people do, that addiction results from a problem in one of these is to ignore the other two. The role of the mind is often forgotten, but as you've seen in these pages and hopefully experienced in your own life, the mind is the key, both in developing an addictive relationship with food and in taking control.

WHAT YOU CAN DO

- *Dip into this book* from time to time to remind yourself of things you've discovered here. You might want to mark passages or write notes for yourself in a journal.

- *Stay involved.* Most things in life require maintenance. You don't just wash your hair once to have clean hair, and you don't go to work once to have a career. You don't pay your rent or mortgage once in order to live where you live, and you don't speak to someone once in order to have a relationship with them. Why should your relationship with food be any different?

You've now discovered the ways of thinking that get you stuck, traps that mean you are unable to make lasting changes in your eating habits. It's not that you don't fall into these traps ever again, it's that you learn the skill of getting out of them fast. You get used to readjusting your frame of mind.

It's very common for people to take things for granted. They make some changes, then these changes become the norm and they tend to forget how things were before those changes were made. If you deliberately remember your motivation and put some thought into it from time to time, your success will last and even improve.

- *Review the three questions* that we explored in the first three chapters whenever you aren't happy with your eating. Remind yourself of the questions and look to see how you are thinking about and using each of these themes. Make the corrections in your thinking and you'll be able to get your eating back into control.

- *A written exercise* can help you to focus on gaining a greater degree of control from time to time. On a sheet of paper, draw three columns and head them with the words, what, why and how.

In the first column, under the what heading, write what it is you want to change, making sure it's as specific as possible. For example, 'to stop eating the leftovers on my children's plates'. In the next column, write down why you want to make this change. In what way will your life be better if you don't eat the leftovers? Remember to find reasons other than weight loss. Finally, write down how you are going to make this change. You might, for example, make a note to buy small containers so that the left-over food can be saved. There's a very good chance that something about accepting your addictive desire to eat would fit in this column.

After you've done this exercise on paper a few times, you'll be able to zip through it in your head whenever you need to.

■ *Whenever you see models* in magazines or beauty shows, remember that they weigh less than the clinical criteria for anorexia nervosa. Many (perhaps most) have eating disorders which means that food is a source of distress for them, and many have had cosmetic surgery, having rib bones removed for example.

■ *If you are a parent*, please note that this book is written for adults, and not for children. It's probably not wise to expect children to make adult choices, as children aren't capable of doing so and nor should they be. Children need to have some choices made for them and need good role models to follow.

Sally's Story

I'm 39, I'm married and I have always worked as a fashion buyer, which I absolutely love. I used to diet a lot when I was in my teens and twenties and that seemed to work quite well, but over the last ten years or so I found it impossible to diet and I ended up feeling rather despondent about it all. I thought that the Eating Less course would help me to get back to dieting again, but I think it's been better than that.

This course was proof to me that I could do something I always had wanted: to make some kind of change so that dieting became unnecessary. I always knew it was a mind thing as much as anything else, but the course helped me to see a lot of things more clearly. In particular, looking at the problem of these two incompatible things: knowing you want to eat better, to eat more fruit and vegetables, and you're absolutely convinced in your mind that you'd feel so much fitter and better – and then half an hour later you're eating the wrong thing. Just because you've just got to have that slice of cake or whatever.

Resolving the conflict between these is something most people don't even begin to do. It's about knowing that by eating better you're actually taking care of yourself. That for me was the essence of the course. I do eat much better now, and especially I eat more fruit and vegetables.

I've had to learn to deal with all the comments about the lost weight, but people seem to have settled about it now and I can just carry on in peace. Although I am aware that I need to keep making an effort with regard to what and when I eat, and although I am sometimes more successful than others, I've really stopped seeing food as anything other than my friend, which is a breath of fresh air!

I go through phases where I eat nothing but fruit until the late afternoon and that works well for me. I wouldn't have been able to do that before I did the course. I go though quite long periods of not eating wheat. It goes in phases. I'm more in tune with what food does to my body now. If I snack on bread and honey I'll get very sleepy half an hour later, and a big meal at lunch time will do the same thing. I feel bloated after I eat white bread.

I hardly ever eat chocolate now, because I don't really enjoy it nearly as much as I think I will. Every now and then I go and buy a chocolate bar, maybe once every few months, and I think 'I want it, so I'm going to have it.' But then I eat it and I think, 'That wasn't such a big deal.' I don't feel guilty about it. I think I'm less hung-up on food now, which is very nice.

RESOURCES

- For information on 'Eating Less' courses lead by the author, send a stamped, self-addressed envelope to: Eating Less, PO Box 2484, London N6 5UX.

- For a copy of my audio cassette in which I talk you through the techniques in this book, send a cheque (made out to Gillian Riley) for Stg£7.50 to: Eating Less, PO Box 2484, London N6 5UX.

- For a fact-sheet on nutritional supplements, send a stamped, self-addressed envelope to me at the same address or send e-mail via the web site.

- Visit my web site: *www.eatingless.com* to find the latest course dates, materials and links.

READING GUIDE

- *The Six Pillars of Self-Esteem* (Bantam, 1994) by Dr Nathaniel Branden is the book I most frequently recommend to my clients. If you think self-esteem is an issue for you, it's well worth investing in this book, perhaps reading it on and off for years, as I do, and especially working on the exercises.

- *Life Strategies* (Hyperion, 1999) by Dr Phil McGraw is a straight-talking, enormously practical self-help book for those who want more general help to get things moving in their lives.

- *Mind Sculpture* (Bantam, 1999) by Ian Robertson provides you with more information on how our brains change physically with the way we think, which we explored in Chapter 4. One of the world's leading researchers on brain rehabilitation, Ian Robertson is a professor at Trinity College, Dublin and University College, London.

- *Eating Less* (Vermilion, 1999) by Gillian Riley takes you over similar ground to 'Beating Overeating' but it's twice as long, so there is considerably more detail.

- *The Optimum Nutrition Bible* (Piatkus, 1997) by Patrick Holford is one of the best books on healthy eating. Holford is the founder of the Institute for Optimum Nutrition in London.

- *Sugar Busters* (Vermilion, 1998) by H. L. Steward & Drs M. C. Bethea, S. S. Andrews & L. A. Balart is the easiest read of the many books available on the glycemic index of carbohydrates.